## Comments Within

*"Even before the barrel was totally pointed at me, I flew towards the cliff. I climbed like a squirrel."*

*Ten-Year-old Ragnhild*

*"........ and that hereafter n-i-g-g-e-r will merely be another way of spelling the word American."*

*Irvin*

*"Be careful who you sleep with, don't pee outside in the cold, and don't mess with Betty......"*

*Max*

*"...... but we called them Broad Ass Marines or Walking Mattresses"*

*Max*

*"We all died in Vietnam. Some of us came back to life dead. If you can't understand that, you weren't part of that war."*

*John*

*"Vietnam was a civil war; Ho Chi Minh was the 'George Washington' of Vietnam, and Kennedy, Johnson, McNamara and Westmoreland where responsible for 59,000 + deaths."*

*Sam*

*"The Tiger Cages were tools of torture ...."*

*Jane*

# KNOW ME

Nancy Curci

**KNOW ME**



*iUniverse books may be ordered through booksellers or by contacting:*

*iUniverse*
*1663 Liberty Drive*
*Bloomington, IN 47403*
*www.iuniverse.com*
*1-800-Authors (1-800-288-4677)*



*Interior Image Credit: Charles Curci*

*ISBN: 978-1-5320-9427-9 (sc)*
*ISBN: 978-1-5320-9428-6 (e)*

*Library of Congress Control Number: 2020904584*

*Print information available on the last page.*

*iUniverse rev. date: 04/14/2020*

# FOREWORD

In a perfect world, there would be no need for a military. In a less than perfect world, there would be a military but it would never be used. In an imperfect world, we would use the military but only when all else failed.

And then there's our world... where we end our young men and women into harm's way, sometimes for noble causes, sometimes not. And they are away from loved ones, and they sweat and are traumatized and maimed and bleed and die. And sometimes we say "thank you for your service."

The military and a democracy are often strange bedfellows. There are times when the political leadership commit forces for reasons the people do not support. Many of us saw the result of this when we returned from Vietnam.

For the most part, those of us who served were above the politics and, in reality, we did not even do it for "Duty, Honor, Country." We did it for the brothers and sisters who stood and marched and sailed and flew with us; for the brotherhood we were absolutely committed to never let down. We did it because we stood shoulder to shoulder with people just like us and we were exhausted, and scared, and lonely together. We formed a sacred bond with the glue of shared extreme experience oftentimes on a knife's edge between living and dying. We were part of something bigger than ourselves.

And we didn't expect gratitude. For me, my service was a privilege, an opportunity to discover what I value and what I was willing to do for those values. What we all lived was oftentimes raw, totally removed from our previous lives as civilians. I believe most veterans feel an internal pride for what they did but keep that pride private. And they know to the very fiber of their being that their service formed the core of who they are today. So, when we hear "thank you for your service," we appreciate those words. But in truth, for me, it comes up short, never crossing the huge gap between those fine sentiments and the intensity of what we actually experienced.

Nancy Curci has bridged that gap. Her formula for gaining access to our secret world was simple. She *asked and listened*. She became a witness to the stories of fear, and pain, and heroism, and sacrifice and pride long locked in boxes because the contents were too intense... incomprehensible outside the brotherhood. She earned her key to those boxes with her honesty, the thousands of miles she traveled, the many hours of compassionate listening and now, with her written words. She has not only shared a treasure trove of stories, but just by listening has done much more. She has healed, affirmed, and validated the men and women of our military, many of whom have been in a limbo of doubt about the significance of their experience. She told me she *had* to tell these stories. It was for her a moral Imperative.

We are creating more veterans every day, and I am hopeful that the wisdom, judgement, courage and compassion forged in the experiences of these men and women will guide our society through the troubled waters ahead. But just as with we veterans of times past, this new breed will be unlikely to come forward with the full breadth of their potential contributions unless we ask and listen and value the priceless nature of what they have to offer us. We need more like Nancy Curci to make this happen.

Read the stories in this book. Try to feel what these veterans felt. Celebrate these heroes among us because if we don't, we will miss the essence of what it means to be a patriot.

Roger Landry Col USAFMC (ret)
Falmouth, Massachusetts

# NOTE FROM THE AUTHOR

I realize that wars have gone on forever, and I see no end to them in the future. I believe that the American military is needed to protect us from those who try to destroy our Constitution, our Bill of Rights, and our democracy. I am an American and believe in my country one hundred percent. I believe we have not evolved to the point of finding new ways of resolving issues. But I hope when you read this book you will feel and understand the price that this one percent pays for defending us and our way of life. They pay it forward. Can we pay it back?

God Bless you and God Bless every veteran who has served this country.

# INTRODUCTION

I'm not brave. I'm not a veteran. I never fought in a war, and I never wore a uniform, unless scout outfits count.

I realized that I was not military material at the age of ten. It was easy to see. I would go to Scout meetings, and after the Pledge of Allegiance, learning how to tie knots and start a fire, I would leave the meeting and go straight to the corner store. There I would snitch a candy bar. I would then proceed to get on the bus to go home. I would jump off without paying, and then, since it was Lent, I would go into the parlor to join my six siblings and mother to say the rosary. I knew then that I was not military mettle.

It was about two decades later I realized that although I did not have what it takes to be part of the military, I did have respect for those who did. My grandfather was in WWI. My uncles were in WWII. My cousin was in Korea, my brother Cornelius was in the Marines, my brother Johnny did three tours in Vietnam, and my son was in Korea at the demilitarized zone in the eighties. They had the guts to go and save someone's life at the risk of their own. Not me.

By the time I really got hit by the awesomeness of these people, these veterans, it was another decade and I was teaching psychology at the local college, and that is where this story begins.

Many of my students were veterans of the wars. I had requested all students to summarize their lives starting from age ten, when they were dreaming of what they would become, to what they have become and to explain why. When the veterans had completed their presentations to the class, on their lives before, during, and after war, I was overwhelmed.

After listening to their experiences, it dawned on me that the recollections of the feet on the ground veterans were very different from the comments from politicians, presidents and the news media.

These veterans told their story with pride, humor, honesty, and pain. I think these stories should be told if only to respect their experiences and for their grandchildren to know the sacrifice that their veterans made for them.

I want to give the veterans a venue to tell how they think, feel and remember about their time in a war zone. Also, I would like to allow the reader to travel through the war times and see how they have been affected today by the past. To show the progress that has been made in human rights, equality, gender differences.

Also, to see if the new weapons made for each new war made a difference in ending wars, making peace, or just ending the precious, precious lives of our children.

I have tried to record from every branch, gender and culture, starting with WWI, WWII, Korean War, and the Vietnam War.

I would very much appreciate your reading this book. So that even though we see, as movies-goers, great make-believe heroes like the Avengers, Superman and Batman and we hang their pictures on our walls, that we never forget how often the real human heroes, called veterans, put themselves and their lives on the line to save us every day.

God Bless You All

# CONTENTS

## As They Remember



## Korean War



## As They Remember

## Vietnam War



### As They Remember

# WORLD WAR I

## Voice of Humanity

*In Flanders Fields*

In Flanders fields the poppies blow
Between the crosses, row on row,
That mark our place; and in the sky
The larks, still bravely singing, fly
Scarce heard amid the guns below.

We are the Dead. Short days ago,
We lived, felt dawn, saw sunset glow,
Loved and were loved, and now we lie
In Flanders fields.

Take up our quarrel with the foe:
To you from failing hands we throw
The torch; be yours to hold it high.
If ye break faith with us who die
We shall not sleep, though poppies grow
In Flanders fields.

*The poem was written by Doctor John McCrae. The red poppies that grew over the graves of the fallen soldiers became a memorial symbol for soldiers who died in that field.*

# CHAPTER 1

*American Life in the early 1900s*

Life was hard for all, with no exceptions. Men worked fifty to sixty hours a week in factories, mines or farms. They had no such things as health insurance, benefits, or pensions. Women pretty much stayed home and worked as many hours as their husbands, or more, with little help from appliances as they have today. Older folks worried about aging because there was no insurance if they got sick, no Social Security, and no weekly visits to the doctor. If they could not work or had no children to support them, they were left to the poor house or religious organizations. Their average life expectancy was around forty five.

Although, America was a young country, it had no concept of young or even "teenage" years. Children, both boys and girls, began working as young as five years old. Young boys would work, in dangerous situations such as in the mines, side by side with the men. They drank, smoked and visited whore houses and aged quickly like their adult co-workers, and they died at very young ages, along with the adult co-workers. There was no place for young children to grow. The minute they could walk and talk there was work to be done. Young girls worked in the mills with no rules for work hours, no safety rules, or say in the work force.

The majority of families lived in homes without a bathtub. Very few had radios, telephones or ice boxes. Many children could not go to school due to families needing their income. This led to one-fifth of children unable to read or write. Personal hygiene was a bath, maybe, once a month and for shampoo one used Borax or egg yolks. They lived in three-generation homes that they rarely owned, ate almost as much lard as chicken and if they wanted to get somewhere, they walked, rode a horse, bike, or hitched a trolley.

The newspaper was the only way most received the worldly news and most could not read it. The only entertainment was a Friday night dancing to a player piano or a phonograph.

Young people going to war in 1914 were accustomed to listening, responding, and obeying. They learned at an early age to sit at the dinner table until they were excused, eat all that was in front of them, whether they enjoyed the taste or not. They were taught to respect, not only it parents but their teachers, police, religious leaders, and their neighbors.

Some of these young people, ages as young as seventeen, knew how to be soldiers. They listened to their military leaders by taking orders without question, to eat what was in front of them, and follow the orders given. They also had never experienced much of the world except their neighborhood, never saw an ocean, and never saw foreign lands.

What difference does a century make?

Just asking.

## The War to End All Wars

Most wars are caused by greed, power, fear, or religion and once in a while, justifiably, for the integrity of mankind. From the beginning of time, wars ended with the victors, the vanquished, and the losers. This leaves the basic need for revenge by the vanquished toward someone, for something, somewhere. So instead of "The War to End All Wars," WW1 became just the first chapter in a continuity of consequential wars.

This war was fueled by outright greed and the pursuit of unlimited power. Greed surfaced in the form of imperialism. It happened when strong European nations competed in conquering smaller weaker nations. Many European countries became jealous that some countries had more territories than others, which in turn caused mistrust and suspicion and became a barricade for partnership. Many disagreements based upon who would control what parts of the world became the primary topic on the tongues of European leaders.

This was also a war of power or nationalism. It was a time that some countries in Western Europe felt they were the best in cultures and interests as opposed to other nations. They made alliances with each other. Something like our "watch my back and I'll watch yours." So, the teams were set, and all that was needed was a catalyst to ignite the flame.

The physical action that kindled the flame on June 28, 1914 was the assassination of the Archduke Franz Ferdinand of Austria. Austria blamed Serbia for the murder of the Archduke and began mobilizing for war in the Balkans. This caused Russia to mobilize, which caused Germany to mobilize, and so on, and so on. The reason America entered the war was Germany's violation of its pledge to suspend unrestricted submarine warfare in the Mediterranean and in the North Atlantic. The Germans were also trying to form an alliance with Mexico in order to invade America.

After devastating costs in human life, including, not only the military, but civilian men, women and children, along with the complete destruction of infrastructure of so many countries, WWI ended. The victors began deciding the fate of the fallen. The major Allied forces were the victors. The major Central Powers were the vanquished. The losers were the children sitting in the rubble along with soldiers who returned home with broken limbs, broken hearts and broken minds, and then there were the dead, the ones who never returned.

Since Germany was viewed as the chief instigator of the war, she was forced to accept full responsibility for reparation. These crushing demands that were put upon the German people left them with feelings of humiliation, along with ruined lives, work, and the basic need for food, safety, and shelter. They appeared to have no direction, no purpose and no hope. The continuation of this level of 'hopelessness' helped fuel the growth of Hitler's Nazism. So even before the healing from WWI could take place, the thinking about revenge was in the making. In place of being "The End of All Wars," history shows it became an instigator for a multitude of the wars that came after.

How can a war be categorized as advantageous or beneficial when it was mainly fueled by greed and power?

Just asking.

# AS THEY REMEMBER

# CHAPTER 2

*"Country Boy" Charles Barger- Heritage Scottish- Army*

## Life Before War

This young country boy definitely started behind the eight ball. Charles Barger's parents were George and Cora Staffelbach, and they left him at five years old at an orphanage.

His father George lived in Galena, Kansas, which was a dangerous and wild place to live in the 1870's. He and his brother were finally charged with and convicted of murder. They spent their lives in jail. His mother gave him up in order to live a life of crime. She ran a bordello, and then, needing more excitement, decided to become a bank robber which lasted seven years. When she was caught, she even posed for pictures showing no regret for what she had done.

Charles was fortunate to be taken in by the Barger family and later was adopted by them. As he grew, he learned about farming and appreciating the land. He became physically fit, responsible, and a hard worker. Charles did not have the opportunity to attend school and learn reading or writing. His life was the farm, and so he was very naive in understanding the world outside his humble environment.

## Life During War

When he decided to enlist in the army, Charles was selected to be an automatic rifle gunner due to his expertise with a rifle. It was six months after enlisting that he found himself a part of the Meuse-Argonne

Offensive. It was there two patrols from his regiment were sent into no man's land to reconnoiter German positions. The Germans sighted them and the two patrols were overpowered by heavy machine gun fire. The patrols held the Germans as long as they could, but they were pinned down and their second lieutenant was seriously wounded. It was then that the lieutenant ordered his men to leave. He told his men to leave him there and try to escape and save themselves.

One soldier from the patrols survived to return to safety. He began explaining that the lieutenant and one other officer were trapped, that they were still alive but wounded. When Barger and his carrier Jesse N. Funk heard of the situation, they volunteered to run the five hundred yards and rescue the officers.

They ran through the heavy machine gun fire. They were twisting and turning and back and forth while trying not to fall, lose the stretcher, or die.

They returned with one officer, laid him down, picked up another stretcher and bravely turned around and headed out for the second officer. When they returned through no man's land, with German soldiers still trying for their hides, to rescue the second lieutenant, they discovered another enlisted man. Believing that they must have angels on their shoulders they went a third time and came back with the third man. It was unbelievable that neither man was hit by enemy fire. It was during this time that the enemy fired high-explosive shells which often contained mustard gas, and gas fumes that lingered for days. No one was without contact, but since Barger did not understand that if he did not report for medical treatment, he would not be allotted a wound chevron for his infliction. This soldier went on, during his military service to fight in many more battles and in doing so received over ten wounds and seven medals of honor from:

America – Medal of Honor- Purple Heart w/ one silver and four bronze oak leaf clusters .Belgium – Order of Leopold, degree of Knight – Croix de guerre w/bronze palm Britain - Military Medal – Army of Occupation of Germany medal France - Medaille Militaire - Croix de guerre w/ three bronze palms and one bronze star Montenegro – Medal for Military Bravery Italy – Croce al Merito de Guerra

At the end of the war, his carrier Funk revealed, "... I used to write letters for him and I got to know him very well. He was scared, too – just as badly scared as any of us, but he had the grit to put it all behind him, and what was more, he'd force it down so far that he could cheer up the other fellows. Believe me, he sure had grit and I'm proud to have been running mate of a man that had so much fight in him as he did."

## Life After War

His life after discharge was no better than the beginning of his life. He tried farming and tried his hand at construction, but had a difficult time with returning to civilian life. He was a member of the American Legion, and members tried to help him find work, but when a chance to re-enlist came up he joined and stayed in the service until 1921. At that time, he married and had a son that he named after himself. He was then hired by the police department in Kansas City. He and his partner were dispatched to where two men were holed up, suspected of murder. His partner was shot in the arm and went down. Charles was shot in the left wrist, right arm, chest and head. With the problems of the effects from mustard gas, shell shock, along with his head wound, life finally took its toll. The two groups that stayed steadfast at his side were the American Legion and Veterans of Foreign Affairs. He said to them, "It's fine to have all the medals, but the trouble is you can't eat them."

The police were called to his house one night. They saw him setting his house on fire and swinging a large knife. A great deal of his body was burned. When he began threatening his second wife. the police tried to arrest him, but he charged them. He was shot. When he reached the hospital, he lasted two days and then died.

No one except the government denied that the breakdown was caused by his military service. A friend who worked for the Kansas City Star wrote, "Yet through the years every effort made by the veterans' organizations to persuade the government that sent him to war to admit responsibility for his mental condition ended in failure. There was no 'proof' in cold language that his suffering was connected with his service. Charles Barger remained a name and a case number."

After reading the number of medals, what do you think?

Just asking.

# CHAPTER 3

## *"Black Death" Henry Johnson – Heritage Black American- Army*

### Life Before War

From pictures I viewed of Henry, he appeared to be a small frame of a man with a smile that crossed his whole face, and his eyes reminded me of a deer in the headlights. There is very little history of Henry's past. He was born in Winston-Salem, North Carolina on July 15, 1892 or 1891. Very few details of his early life are known, including the names of his parents or what his exact age was. His life had been one of financial poverty, and so in his early teens he took off to find his fortune in New York. Being a young black fellow and with times so hard as far as job hunting, he ended up working many menial jobs such as a laborer in a coal yard, soda mixer in a drug store, a chauffeur, and then a job as a redcap porter at the Albany Union Station on Broadway.

### Life During the War

When the United States declared war on Germany in 1917, Henry Johnson, this short, hundred and thirty pounds shy fellow decided to enlist. The regiment belonged to the largely black 93rd Division of the American Expeditionary Force. This regiment was also called the "Harlem Hell Fighters."

He landed in Europe and along with his fellow Hell Fighters he was ready to go and do his duty. It was discovered at that time that the French Fourth Army was in need of more troops. It was U.S. General Pershing who lent the 369th. Pershing explained to the French Commander, that he should be aware, that "black soldiers are inferior to whites." In his opinion they lacked the "civic and professional conscience" and were a "constant menace to the American." The French did not listen to what was being said. They were happy to have support and the 369th who went to the western edge of Argonne Forest where the war was erupting and showed what stuff they were made of.

Henry showed that Pershing was wrong about what the 369th could do. Due to his fierce fighting in the Argonne on May 4, 1918 he was dubbed "Black Death." As the story was told, he and another fellow named Roberts were on sentry duty when German snipers began shooting. The following story is in the words of Henry Johnson, a quiet little black man from New York.

"There isn't much to tell. There wasn't anything so fine about it. Just fought for my life. A rabbit would have done that.

Well, anyway, me and Needham Roberts were on patrol duty on May 15. The corporal wanted to send out two new drafted men on the sentry post for the midnight-to-four job. I told him he was crazy to send untrained men out there and risk the rest of us. I said I'd tackle the job, though I needed sleep.

German snipers had been shooting our way that night, and I told the corporal he wanted men on the job who knew their rifles. He said it was imagination, but anyway he took those men off and left Needham and me on the posts. I went on at midnight. It was moonlight. Roberts was at the next post. At one 'clock a sniper took a crack at me from a bush fifty yards away. Pretty soon there was more firing and when Sergeant Roy Thompson came along, he asked 'What's the matter men, 'You scared?'

No, I ain't scared, I said, I came over here to do my bit and I'll do it. But I was jes' lettin' you know there's liable to be some tall scrappin' around this post tonight'. He laughed and went on and I began to get ready. They'd a box of hand grenades there and I took them out of the box and laid them all in a row where they would be handy. There was about thirty grenades. I guess. I was goin' to bust that Dutch army in pieces if it bothered me.

"Somewhere around two o'clock I heard the Germans cutting our wire out and I called Roberts. When he came, I told him to pass the word to the lieutenant. He had just started off when a snippin' an clippin' of the wires sounded near, so I let go with a hand grenade. There was a yell from a lot of surprised Dutchmen and then they started firing. I hollered to Needham to come back.

"A German grenade got Needham in the arm and in the hip. He was so badly wounded to do any fighting, so I told him to lie in the trench and hand me up the grenades.

"Keep your nerve I told him. All the Dutchmen in the woods are at us, but keep your cool and we'll lick'em. Roberts crawled into the dugout. Some of the shots got me, one clipped my head, another my lip, another my hand, some in my side and another smashed my left foot so bad that I have a silver plate holding it up now.

"The Germans came from all sides. Roberts kept handing me grenades, and I kept throwing them, and the Dutchmen kept squealing, but jes' the same they kept comin' on. When the grenades were all gone, I started in with my rifle. That was alright until I shoved in an American cartridge clip - it was a French gun - and it jammed. There was nothing to do but use my rifle as a club and jump into them. I banged them on the dome and the side and everywhere I could land until the butt of my rifle busted. One of the Germans hollered, 'Rush him! Rush him!' I decided to do some rushing myself. I grabbed my French bolo knife and slashed in a million directions. Each slash meant something, believe me. I wasn't doing exercises, let me tell you. I picked out an officer, a lieutenant, I guess he was. I got him and got some more of them. They knocked me around considerably and whanged me on the head, but I always managed to get back on my feet. There was one guy who bothered me. He climbed on my back and I had some job shaking him off and pitching him over my head. I then struck him in the ribs with my bolo. I struck one guy in the stomach and he yelled in good New York talk: 'That black nigger got me'. I was still banging them when my crowd came up and saved me and beat the Germans off. That fight lasted about an hour. That's about all. There wasn't so much to it."

## Life After the War

W. Allison Sweeney who was the author of The American Negro in the World War and had written about Henry, stated, "Right, there was not much to it, excepting that next morning the Americans found four German bodies with plentiful indications that at least thirty-two others had been put on the casualty list and several of the German dead probably had been dragged back by their comrades. Thirty-eight bombs were found, besides rifles, bayonets and revolvers".

A southern writer, named Irvin S. Cobb, for the Saturday Evening Post wrote "…….that as a result of what our black soldiers are going to do in this war, a word that has been uttered billions of times in our country, sometime in derision, sometime in hate, sometime in all kindness – but which I assure never fell on black ears but it left behind a sting for the heart, is going to have a new meaning for all of us, South and North too, and that hereafter n-i-g-g-e-r will merely be another way of spelling the word American."

Although, stated by Teddy Roosevelt that Johnson was "One of the five bravest Americans to serve in the war," Even though his picture was on victory stamps, even though his picture was on army recruiting materials, there never was mention of his wounds. Due to this mishap of paperwork without government benefits Henry tried to go back to work. The physical and psychological pain of twenty wounds was simply too much for Henry. He began using alcohol for a self-medication. He lost his wife, his children and his job. Henry died a pauper in 1929. He was old and lost and dead at thirty-two years old.

Henry received France's Croix de Guerre with star and bronze palm while he was alive. In 1996 he was awarded the Purple Heart. In 2002 The US military awarded him the Distinguished Service Cross. In 2015 in a posthumous ceremony he received the Medal of Honor from President Barack Obama.

How much, since 1919, do you believe has changed?

Just asking.

# CHAPTER 4

*"Undocumented Immigrant" - Marcelino Serna- Heritage Mexican - Army*

## Life Before the War

Marcelino was a soft spoken undocumented Mexican. His features presented a young man with dark eyes, strong cheek bones, a proud stance, and strong work hands. By appearance alone one could tell he was a hard worker.

He was born into poverty in a small mining camp near Chihuahua, Mexico. He grew up with little to call his own, let alone enough food or shelter. So, when he was old enough to work, he began searching. When he turned nineteen, he decided, with the job market still zero to none, in order to make a living he would need to look at other options. So, in 1916 this young Mexican gave up home and family and headed to America, without knowing his future but believing anything would be better than the life he was living.

He was able to cross the border and within a short period found himself a job as maintenance worker. From there he was hired to work in a beet field in Denver. Since he was young and healthy the beet field with a higher wage was the right job for him. This is where his life choices made the difference in the rest of his life.

It was 1917 and the United States declared war on Germany. At the same time, our young Mexican beet worker was picked up. When they found he was an undocumented worker, he made a deal. He would join the Army in lieu of being deported. Understanding the need for young men, even though he did not speak English, they decided to take him up on his offer. They immediately took Marcelino to the recruitment center.

## Life During the War

With a three-week training period he was off to Europe. Once he landed in Europe it was discovered that he spoke little English and was not an American citizen, he was told he could return home. He refused. He had made a deal and he would follow through. He felt now he had a purpose.

As the war progressed and his unit was attacked by heavy enemy fire, and when many of his brothers had been shot and were dying around him, he decided to offer himself to search out the enemy. He was alone, and he felt tense and scared with every step, but continued until he found the machine gun. He crawled as close to the ground as a body can get, getting as close as he could get to the machine gun opening. He quietly pulled the pin on his first grenade and threw it, ending up with six of the enemy killed and eight more came out with their hands up.

He began to feel he worked best alone and so when an enemy sniper appeared, again he offered himself to follow and find the German nest. From a distance, he followed the sniper until he found the destination. He then scouted the surroundings and with a determined plan which began with throwing grenades and charged the enemy position. He continued to move from one position to another so many times that the enemy thought they were surrounded. This time he took twenty-four prisoners and killed twenty-six. When the American soldiers arrived and suggested to just shoot them on the spot, this naïve, humble soldier with a language barrier refused because the rules went against it.

Marcelino's luck ran out just a few days before the end of the war. He was doing his job, as he had done since the time he enlisted, when a sniper shot him. He was hit in both legs. When the Armistice was signed, he was in a French hospital recuperating.

Medals that this young Mexican undocumented immigrant received:

American – Distinguished Service Cross, Two Purple Hearts. France – Two Croix de Guerre with palms, St. Mihiel Medal, Verdun Medal, Victory medal with five stars, Victory medal with three bars. Italy – Croe al Merito di Guerra

## Life After the War

Marcelino retired from the service and returned to El Paso, Texas. First, he found work in a packing company for a short period and then he lucked out by working in the quartermaster's department at Fort Bliss. He became a member of the Veterans of Foreign Wars, and would take part in the military parades.

He married Simona Jiménez, and they had six children. out of the six only two of their children survived to adulthood. Marcelino became a U.S. citizen in 1924 and continued to work as a city truck driver, a civil service employee at Fort Bliss.

Marcelino Serna died in 1992 in El Paso, Texas, with full military honors and was buried at Fort Bliss National Cemetery.

Many questioned why, with all the medals that Marcelino had received, he did not receive the Congressional Medal of Honor. Marcelino had stated at one time that his superior officers refused to recommend him for the honor because he was too low in rank and because his English skills were not proficient enough to warrant a promotion. Others claimed it was because of racial prejudice.

Why do you think we always get one bad superior apple in the bunch?

Just asking.

# CHAPTER 5

*"Not Allowed" Ellen N. La Motte-Heritage French -Nurse*

## Life Before the War

Ellen was born to a very influential family. She was able to indulge in the finer things of life along with the opportunity to attend a very prestigious private girls' school.

It was in 1898 that Ellen decided to enlist in schooling for nursing. Due to many objections from her parents, she was unable to complete her chosen profession until 1902. After her graduation, she traveled to Italy and worked as a private nurse. It was a few years later that she ended up in Paris, France. She was a socialist and self-proclaimed anarchist; she challenged America's social order. As a lesbian she declared herself willing to withstand social censure to be with the woman she loved for forty-five years.

In Paris she decided to join the American Ambulance Service and became a part of WWI. Soon after, instead of taking a safe job at the Paris Hospital she decided she would take the opportunity to join a French private nursing hospital in Belgium. She moved on from being an ambulance driver to that of a nurse on the front lines with few miles between her and the enemy. It was there that she started a diary that later became the book that was published in 1916 and was banned in America in 1918 as it was believed it would damage the public morale. Her book "The Backwash of War" was based on her experience on the front lines during WWI. Her honesty and straight forward account of the damage of war to the human soul, body and mind was considered unpatriotic and so it was not released until 1934. Her book is about the realness of war in a very blunt and to the point way. It was meant to open the public's eyes not damage their morale. The backwash is left after the tides of the oceans leave the shore. It is the leftover refuse of the sea. That is what I believe Ellen was talking about; The wasted human leftovers of war.

## Life During the War

Pieces of Ellen's introduction about war state that up and down the long-reaching kilometers of the front there were actions, and moments of intense fright having produced glorious deeds of valor, courage, devotion, and nobility. But when there is no action then there is a stagnant place that churns up the wake of mighty, moving forces. This is the Backwash of War. It is very ugly. There are many little lives foaming up in the backwash. They are loosened by the sweeping current, and float to the surface, detached from their environment, and one glimpses them as weak, hideous and repellent.

She tells of one soldier who could take it no longer. "He fired a revolver up through the roof of his mouth, but he made a terrible mess of it. The ball tore out of his left eye, and then lodged somewhere under his skull, so they bundled him up and put him into an ambulance and carried him cursing and screaming to the nearest field hospital. The journey was made in double-quick time, over rough Belgian roads. To save his life, he must reach the hospital without delay, and if he was bounced to death jolting along at breakneck speed, it did not matter. That was understood. He was a deserter, and discipline must be maintained. Since he had failed in the job, his life must be saved, he must be nursed back to health, until he is well enough to be stood up against a wall and shot. This is War.

"At the hospital, he behaved abominably. Upon the operating table he shouted and screamed and threw himself side to side. It took four or five orderlies to hold him in position. During this commotion, his left eye rolled about loosely upon his cheek, and from the bleeding mouth he shot great clots of stagnant blood, caring not where they fell. Truly it was disgusting.

"At last they said he was ready. During his struggles they had broken out two big teeth with a mouth gag, and that added a little more blood to the blood already choking him. The Medecin Major did a very skillful operation. He trephined the skull, extracted the bullet that had lodged beneath it, and bounced back in place that erratic eye.

He was so different from the other patients, who wanted to live. It was a joy to nurse them. This was the Salle of the Grands Blesses, those most seriously wounded. By expert surgery, expert nurses. Some of these were to be returned to their homes again, reformed, mutilated for life, a burden to themselves and to society; others were to be nursed back to health, to a point at which they could again shoulder eighty pounds of marching kit, and be torn to pieces again on the firing line. It was pleasure to nurse such as these. It called forth all one's skill, all one's humanity. But to nurse back to health a man who was to be court-martialed and shot, truly that seemed a dead-end occupation."

Ellen went on to tell about other patients on her ward. She said, "Here lay Felix, asleep. Poor, querulous, feeble- minded Felix, with a foul fistula, which filled the whole ward with its odour. In one sleeping hand lay his little round mirror, in the other, he clutched his comb. With daylight, he would trim and comb his moustache his poor, little drooping moustache, and twirl the ends of it.

"In bed two, on the right, lay Alexandre, asleep. He received the Medaille Militaire for bravery. He was better now, and that day he asked for permission to smoke. He was refused, saying that it would disturb the other patients. Yet after the doctor had gone, Alexandre had produced a cigarette and lighted it, defying the all from behind his Medaille Militaire. The patient in the next bed had become violently nauseated in consequence, yet Alexandre had smoked on, secure in his medal. How much honor lay in that?

"Beyond lay Alphonse, drugged with morphia, after an intolerable day. That morning he had received a package from home, a dozen pears. He had eaten them all, one after the other, though his companions in the beds adjacent looked on with hungry, longing eyes. He offered not one, to either side of him. After his gorge, he became violently ill, and demanded the basin in which to unload his surcharged stomach.

"There was Hippolyte, who needed his appendicitis removed, He was not ill and his dirty jokes filled the ward, provoking laughter, even from dying Marius. How filthy had been his jokes - how they had been matched and beaten by other jokes of others. How filthy they all were, when they talked with each other."

She wondered wherein lay the difference between the patients. Was it all a dead-end occupation, nursing back to health men to be patched up and returned to the trenches, or a man to be patched up, court-martialed and shot? She believed the difference was in the ideals.

"One had no ideals. The others had ideals, and fought for them. Yet had they? Poor selfish Alexandre, poor vain Felix, poor gluttonous Alphonse, poor filthy Hippolyte- was it possible that each cherished ideals, hidden beneath?

What do you think?

Just asking.

## Questions

The following questions were influenced by changes in cultural prejudices, media responsibility, political hyperbole, and government goals throughout the past hundred years. Following the questions are anecdotal and unique responses provided by veterans from WWl to the Vietnam War. WWI responses came through research material by the author.

## WWl Questions and answers:

1. What was the reason for war?
   Greed (imperialism) and Power (nationalism).
2. What was the role of the black soldier?
   He was perceived as inferior and mostly assigned to menial work as dock loader, kitchen help, or janitor. More than 200,000 African Americans served in WWI, but only about 11 percent of them were in combat forces. The rest were put in labor units,

loading cargo, building roads, and digging ditches. They served in segregated divisions (the 92nd and 93rd) and trained separately from Caucasians.

3. What was the role of women?

   In 1914 the public opinion about women as far as their being a part of the military was negative. It was unheard of. Their role was to keep the home fires burning, or as the saying went "keep them barefoot and pregnant." That about said it all. But in spite of this attitude nurses served overseas, although they served without rank. The US Army refused to enlist women officially, relying on them as contract employees and civilian volunteers. If women became engaged in combat it would undermine the status quo which was only those who fought for their nation (men) had the right for citizenship and the right to vote. Wives were not allowed in the front lines to see their loved ones, but prostitutes were. They would cheer the men up but wives might make them melancholy.

   Do you wonder why there was such a need for penicillin? Just asking.

4. What was the role of gays and lesbians?

   In America, homosexuals committing a "crime against nature" would end up with a court martial or blanketed. Blanketed meant throw a blanket over them and then beat the crap out of them. This type of thinking led to many good officers and enlisted men, who were willing to fight for their country, being given long jail sentences, and/or dishonorable discharge. This seemed to be the mindset of many countries when the war broke out in 1914.

5. What was the role of Native American Indians?

   The Choctaw Indians were the first code talkers and could interpret enemy communications. Choctaw tribe members formed the Oklahoma National Guard unit who used an extremely complex language that the Germans could not translate. The eight Choctaw men, and others who joined them, became known as the Choctaw Code Talkers. Even though the

U.S. government did not grant Native Americans citizenship until 1924, nearly 13,000 of them served in WWI.

6. What was the role of the media?
   Basically, the news was reported through the radio or the weekly paper. The media and the public were in support of the war.
7. What is post-traumatic stress disorder?
   In WWl it was called "shell shock" and was seldom treated. The individual was seen as acting coward-like and would be forced back into the fighting field. Millions of soldiers suffered "shell shock" due to the horrors of trench warfare. Shell shocked men often had uncontrollable diarrhea, couldn't sleep, stopped speaking, whimpered for hours, and twitched uncontrollably. While some soldiers recovered, others suffered for the rest of their lives'. Many were given a guilt trip and told that they were letting their fellow soldiers down.
8. What would you tell young people today about joining the service?
   Unable to answer for WW l veterans.
9. What was the average age for recruits?
   The 'required' age was eighteen to thirty-five, but all armies in the Great War used 'kid soldiers'. In the beginning of the war the underage were as young as twelve. At the end of the war these poorly trained children were found in the trenches where they mingled with the older troops - dead.
10. Would you do it again?
    Unable to answer for WWI veterans.

## Letter Home

***Letter Home from WWI Veteran*** *David Ker the day before the attack on Saint-Michael in France.*

"Tomorrow the first totally American drive commences, and it gives me inexpressible joy and pride to know that I shall be present to do my share. Should I go under, therefore, I want you to know that I went without any terror of death and that my chief worry is the grief my death will bring to those so dear to me.

Since having found myself and Mary, there has been much to make life sweet and glorious, but death, while distasteful, is in no way terrible.

I feel wonderfully strong to do my share well, and for my sake you must try to drown your sorrow in the pride and satisfaction and the knowledge that I died well in so clean a cause, as is ours, should bring to you. Remember how proud I have always been of your pluck, keep Elizabeth's future in mind, and don't permit my death to bow your head.

My personal belongings will all be sent to you. Your good taste will tell you which to send to Mary. May God bless and keep you, dear heart, and be kind to little Elizabeth, and those I love so well.

David

The end."

## Weapons Used in WWI

**Trench Warfare** which was a dirt trench that went along the Western Front. It was infested with rats, lice, along with being waterlogged and muddy. These men fought, lived, ate, slept and died in the filth of these trenches. The diseases that caused many losses even before the battle started were infection caused by louse feces, inflammation of the kidneys and foot infections that caused swelling of the feet when exposed to long periods of dampness and cold, sometimes causing the need for amputation. Some called the time in the trenches "**Hell on Earth**".

**Flame Thrower.** was worse than any instrument of torture ever seen in any horror movie. It could simply incinerate a human in seconds. A young soldier, who was fighting in the trenches, looked over the edge, and saw a German soldier with a canister on his back and a hose that shot fire. All he could he see was his buddies being burnt alive. The media, politicians, and military called foul. They called the flame thrower an inhumane project of the German Mind but before the war ended more than just Germany was using them.

**Poison Gasses** -Lachrymator - tear gas. This caused temporary blindness and serious irritation to the nose and throat of the victims. Chlorine gas mixes with moisture in the air so it will attack the eyes and lungs. Suffocating gasses - caused severe edema of the lungs and death from asphyxiation. It was almost odorless and caused serious blisters both internally and externally.

**Fighter Planes** –The pilots did not have parachutes. The planes were made of thin strips of wood, linen cloth and wire. The bombs were hand dropped over enemy territory. The bomb was really hand held and needed precision in dropping it in order to hit the target. A machine gun was eventually mounted on the bi-plane to fight enemy aircraft. These particular battles were called "dogfights". The pilot had to turn off the plane's engine from time to time so it would not stall when the plane turned quickly in the air. When the pilot restarted his engine midair, it sounded like dogs barking hence the term "Dogfights"

**Communication** was improved from dogs and messenger pigeons, which was the main form of communication until the use of telegraph, Morse code, radio, and the Choctaw Indian language known as Code Talking. Communication between family and the enlisted could take months to be delivered. Communication between husband and wife were a bit strange. Wives were not allowed to visit their husbands during war time because it might lower the soldier's morale, but the soldiers could be cheered up by local prostitutes. It was also thought communication through letters, from loved ones, would make the soldiers melancholy so, they also were discouraged.

What do you think?
Just asking.

# WORLD WAR II

**Humanity**

When greed sups with the devil
And principles are shed
When power is corrupted
And truth stands on its head
When fear pervades the confused mind
And fools are easy led
When reason is a prisoner
The bell tolls for the dead

*Tom Walker served in the Royal Navy in World War Two*

# CHAPTER 6

## *American Life in the Early 1940s*

For many, it was a much slower time in the early forties. It was steadier and safer when the veterans of WWII were growing up in America. It was a time when you would stop and say hi to a neighbor. If you needed help clearing a field or delivering a package to little old Mr. Jones, support was there. Children had time to run free, in their hand-me-down faded overalls, and catch grasshoppers, go fishing in the river, with a string, a worm, and a hook, or play stickball in the town's old sand lot. There was more fresh air to breath and less to fear than in today's environment.

It was a time in America when communication came in the form of the daily newspaper and a local radio station. Segregated buses and trains were the basic form of travel, and three- to five-party lines were how telephones operated. These soon-to-be veterans were hard working from the time they could stand, until the time they went to school and after school they came home and went right back to work.

They asked for little and got just that. Perhaps an orange for Christmas or a hot meal for Thanksgiving, a piece of cake for birthdays. Many of these veterans-to-be were born to immigrant parents and had not yet explored outside their safe cultural haven. So young, so inexperienced, so beautifully naïve of the world they were about to enter.

## WWII Begins

It has been twenty years since WWI ended. The European children of that war have grown. They are the children who have lived through the war. They did not comprehend the reason for the war, but did experience the emotion, confusion, loss and fear that the war created. They were the ones who lived through the penalty of war.

These children were left with little to rebuild their lives. The devastation and destabilization were felt throughout Europe. The destruction was something the existing world population had never experienced.

The German youth had to live with the crushing demands and limitations that were imposed upon them, at the end of World War One. There was a great resentment over the harsh terms demanded by the Versailles Treaty. The young grew "frustrated" over twenty years and were anxious to follow someone who could lead them out of despair and upward toward feelings of pride in themselves and their country again and to take part in the world as equals. This need for direction, and hope for a better life would fuel the fire for the Nazi Party and its leader Adolph Hitler.

WWII was a war of hate and revenge. Hatred is what Hitler taught the youth of Germany. He taught them to hate all humans except Germans. He considered them less than his conceived image of ideal. He hated the Jews, their young, old, rich and poor. He blamed the Jews primarily for the loss of the WWI and he blamed them for the position Germany was presently in.

Revenge was the second reason for instigating the war. Hitler was obsessed with the thought that he was a supreme leader and that the German "race" was a superior race. He wanted a war in order to gain back the territory and power that was taken during the last war. He was so overwhelmed with the idea that the pure German race which he called "Aryan" would need more living space for the perfect ethnicity to expand. He would need to retrieve territory taken in the last war and he would need to exterminate Jews.

The reason America entered the war was Japan attacked Pearl

Harbor, and then Germany declared war on America. America entered the war fighting the two fronts: Japan in the Pacific and Germany in the West.

Germany surrendered May 8, 1945. Their "brave" leader Hitler committed suicide on April 30 in Berlin. The Allies were the victors in the Pacific with the dropping of the Atom Bomb on Hiroshima, Japan, August 6, 1945. In order to assure Japan's surrender, another bomb was dropped on Nagasaki. Three days later, Japan surrendered.

After much pain, destruction, and death WWII ended, and the victors began deciding the fate of the fallen. The major Allied Forces were America, Britain, Russia and France, they were the victors. The Major Axis Forces were Germany, Italy and Japan; they were the vanquished. Again, it is the children who are the losers, who will sit in the rubble of their lives and wait and plan for another twenty years.

The victors decided that Germany would be divided into four occupation zones. These zones to be controlled by Britain, America, France and the Soviet Union.

There were no treaties imposed on Germany and no economic punishment on the German people as in WWI. Punishment was on individuals for their actions (Nuremberg Trials).

With the end of the war there was a global shift in the power which left Russia and America the superpowers. Russia believed in communism, and America believed in capitalism/democracy. The difference in beliefs and ideology that they both held with an almost religious-like certainty was about to cause a major problem. Before the ink was dry ending WWII the word "containment" was in the works and a new conflict was about to begin.

# AS THEY REMEMBER

# CHAPTER 7

*"Child of War" Ragnhild Munck –- Heritage Danish - 10 year old child*

## Life Before the War

I found a seat. I could tell at once I was lucky to have picked the seat next to her. She was a tall, blond, Danish woman. She spoke with a mild but convincing tone. By her stance, manners and our conversation, I realized she was very much an independent woman who was strong willed and who was in charge of her life.

At the beginning of our conversation we talked about interests, family, and life in general. Her name was Ragnhild and she told me she was born in Denmark, of a family of five, and she was nine when the Germans invaded her country. We needed to stop conversing since the workshop began. We made a date to have lunch and finish our conversation, since I had told her about this book and I would very much like to interview her.

A week later I am sitting at a Danish lunch. Ragnhild had set a wonderful table. Since I'm a meat and potato person, I was concerned when I saw this table spread with pickled herring, smoked salmon and trout. There were meats, cheeses and usually beer or aquavit to go with. She said if I had time to linger there was coffee and cookies. I had no need to be concerned for the food was great and I did linger for coffee and cookies. She had lit two candles and it was in this calming atmosphere that she began to tell me her story.

## Life During the War

"On April 9, 1940 the German army crossed the border with Denmark and we were at war. I was nine years old and lived with my parents and three siblings in the seaside hotel my parents were running. Almost immediately a small German unit took over a house on the premise. We children were told to ignore the Germans, not even look at them when passing. They were the enemy. At first, we hardly saw them. Our daily life continued much the same. We rode the school bus to town every day, and the first summer we played around the hotel and on the beach undisturbed. Except for this one time. Next to the hotel was a large green field protected against the west wind by the wooded hillside with large trees. At the end of the field a steep cliff rose almost vertical out of the fjord. It was dangerous to climb it because of frequent slides, and we were forbidden to do so.

"One Sunday, I walked along the water's edge picking up shells and pebbles and weeds to play with. When I had enough in my apron pocket and was just about to turn around to head home, I froze in my tracks. There was the most horrible noise coming from somewhere, an earsplitting roar that made me stand still and just turn my head in that direction. There, from under the trees, came a monster vehicle with a long, long canon. It bobbed up and down a bit over the uneven ground as it slowly moved in my direction. Even before the barrel was totally pointed at me, I flew towards the cliff. I climbed like a squirrel, grasping whatever I could get a hold of. I reached the top, caught my breath and ran as fast as I could. I told my father how I got away. Climbing the dangerous cliff saved me. That was the first run-in with the enemy."

Ragnhild was so calm in telling her story that I took another piece of Danish bread and a nice piece of cheese, sat back in my chair and just let her continue. She said, "Gradually more and more soldiers were stationed in Denmark. Father had to give up one of the main halls in the hotel. Our school had to give up the large gym, and a fence was installed right down the middle of the playground. We had to give up some classrooms and we saw more and more German soldiers in the streets. The boys thought of ways to irritate or make fun of the soldiers. They would shout 'Bedst

Hitler and Himler' which in Danish means that the best Hitler could do was to fantasize about victory. Best, Hitler, and Himler were names of infamous Germans.

"We girls would enjoy crocheting caps in red, white, and blue. The exact image of the marks on the English spitfires flying over Denmark to drop ammunition to the resistance movement. The caps were finally outlawed."

Ragnhild, then explained, "The winters were bitterly cold. We experienced 30 degrees below zero and lots of snow. It was at this time that all Danish police were rounded up and sent to concentration camps, if they did not manage to escape capture and go underground. In October of '43' the hunt for the Danish Jews started, but the Rabbi in Copenhagen had been warned beforehand through one of our politicians, Hans Hedtoft. He had been told by a high-ranking German officer what was about to happen. So approximately seven-thousand Danish Jews went into hiding and were helped across to Sweden in small boats."

We went back to talk about her living space in the hotel. "Around our hotel", she said, "They had put barbed wire and tank traps and insisted that every person entering or leaving the hotel had an identifying card. That meant that my sister Bodil and I every morning had to show our ID to get out to catch the school bus. One morning the bus was early or we were late. Coming around the corner we saw the bus and we started running. The driver saw us and waited for us. Bodil flew past the guard without showing her ID, so I did the same while the guard lowered his gun and shouted 'STOP! Do I have to shoot?' Very foolishly I shouted 'Go ahead,' and luckily, he did not. When we got home, Bodil complained to father: 'Those stupid Germans. They see us every morning. So, why do we have to stop? They know we have to catch the bus!' But father was not pleased. He became very serious and told us to always stop and show our ID. He said some of the soldiers were quite desperate, for they knew they might be shipped off to fight the Russian army soon. Some had already lost fathers, brothers, and family members at home."

Ragnhild continued, "There was one day that I will never forget. We were on our way home from school and we passed the carriage house. We saw a soldier standing guard next to what looked like a human being lying at the side of the road covered with a blanket. When we got into the kitchen, we asked the cook if she knew what happened. She told us that one of the young soldiers had shot himself and that it was too bad that no one had shot Hitler instead. She said some of these soldiers were young boys who just came out of high school."

Another cup of coffee, while imagining myself in the middle of WWII and being this girl in that environment at the age of 10-11. She was telling the story ever so calmly that I really could imagine myself in her words. She continued, "One day while we sat in the kitchen having our afternoon tea, we heard father speak in a very loud voice. Apparently, a sergeant had gone into the private loft where he had no business, and father had caught him in the act. When the sergeant shouted at father that he did what he pleased, father told him in no uncertain terms that he would report him to the Commandant. The sergeant clicked his heals and left with a sheepish look on his face. He obviously had not expected father to raise his voice. Father was usually calm and a man of few words. That is why we felt safe when he was near. We really enjoyed that altercation. Mother was his opposite. She had a fierce temper and would dare to tell any soldier who came into her kitchen to, Get Out!"

Then there was the story that had me sit up straight and no longer in a calm state. Ragnhild said, "One afternoon mother and I came into the kitchen to make tea. On a large, black stove was a huge coffee machine and next to it was a pot where something was being heated up as steam came out of it. She said something like, 'Who is heating coffee this time of day.' She then grabbed the pot and poured the contents up into the big coffee machine. At that exact moment the door opened from the foyer. A sergeant appeared and saw what mother had done and he pulled out his revolver. He yelled 'Sind Sie Verruckt? Das war glühwein! Which means: 'Are you mad, that was red wine'? He then pointed his gun right at her. I moved a couple of steps so I would be in front of my mother. I was sure he would not shoot at me. I was only eleven. I was not so sure he would not shoot mother. All of a sudden, a new officer came in and pushed the sergeant aside and gave him orders. Then he turned to mother and said, 'Entschuldigen Sie gnadige Frau. Wir wunchen keine Unglucksfalle. Passen Sie auf. Die Krieg wird Ja scon Zu Ende sein!' (So sorry, Madam, please be careful. We do not want any accidents. The war will soon be over!) When I told father what had happened, mother tried to downplay it. Father told her if she was not careful and could not control herself, we might lose our mother and he would lose his wife. He was very serious. That same evening, I came into the kitchen and found mother sitting in a chair, obviously shaken. When I asked her what happened, she said she had gone out in the foyer and stood at the foot of the stairs while the cook went up to her room. She wanted to make sure no soldiers approached her. Father saw her and went out to tell her come back into the kitchen and managed to pull her back just before a two-hundred-pound sack with sand was thrown down from the second floor. It hit the floor where she had stood and all the sand came out. It would probably have killed her, had father not rescued her in time."

Ragnhild went on to say, "Although we children lived in the hotel and were more and more aware of the problems the war created, we really did not understand how awful the situation was for our parents and all the grownups. We did feel safe in our home and with our parents. The war was becoming a part of our daily life with all the tanks, wire, and soldiers. Father knew it was getting worse and so he told us we would have to move from the hotel."

## Life After the War

We were coming to a close and she said, "Since I am writing my own story about my time in the war, I hope I shared enough for you to use in your story. I must keep some stories for my readers when it is published." She did go a bit further in saying, "The war and the German occupation lasted five years from the time I was nine until I was fourteen. The two hotels my parents ran were taken over. One was taken by the Germans and the other was used to house refugees; some had marched from as far away as Lithuania. My family spent the last months of the war in a summer house of a relative. Back then, in WWII there was no phrase like PTSD. But I am still reminded of that tank every time a big truck comes roaring past me."

Her last words were, "We managed to survive. I now live a happy life in U.S. and visit Denmark once a year." There is a saying "you can't go home again," but even that, Ragnhild challenges. She says, "You Can Go Home Again, this summer I have booked three nights at the hotel where I was born, one of the most beautiful spots on earth."

I do not know how much energy Ragnhild had left, but I was just exhausted from listening. I do not know if I would be brave enough to, at the age of nine to tell a German guide with a rifle "go ahead," or at the age of eleven stand in front of my mother so she would not get shot. I thanked her for her time and her generous gift of tales from her book "One Life, Many Lives"

Would you be that brave?

Just asking.

## Questions

1. Why do we have war?
   "Some men want power and do not care about the cost of human lives. If we want freedom, we have to fight back the best way we can."
2. What was the role of women?
   "In WWII in Denmark they helped hide people who went underground and helped printing illegal newspapers, as normal newspapers were censored by the Germans."
3. What was the role of gay/lesbians?
   "Being gay or lesbian was never an issue, never a problem for anybody in Denmark while I lived there."
4. Role of the media
   "In Denmark the papers and radio were censored by the Germans, therefore the illegal papers were our media. We had a 'free' radio newscast from England, but had to listen to it without the Germans finding out."

5. What would you tell young children about joining the service?
"Do research and interviews to find out if you want to join. I was three years in the Danish Home Guard. We were somewhat afraid the Russians might invade us. They occupied one small island for up to ten months after the war was over. The Soviet was a threat, for instance there were 400 Polish officers who spoke fluent Danish. You wonder why!!"

# CHAPTER 8

*Abby "Gutsy Gunner" Johnson – Heritage - French-Air Force*

## Life Before the War

Abby was a fifteen-year-old kid when he tried to join the Air Force. It was crazy youth that made him want to join. He said, "My brother had just joined, and I wanted to beat him to the war and a tail gunner in a Wellington lull would do the job. That was when I received the shock of my life. I was told I was Canadian not an American. I went as an American to join the service and came out as a visitor from the north. It was never told to me that when I was about a year old my family moved to Massachusetts, USA. So off to Canada I went. We were all on the same side anyway.

"I was taught perseverance from my dad, who was a carpenter and who taught me to keep it simple, go slow, keep it steady, aim for perfection and you won't have to do the job twice. I became a very good carpenter. It is what I taught my son and he taught his. It was that training that helped me become such a good tail gunner. Go slow, stay steady, fire, perfection."

## Life During the War

Know how today you can sit on the couch and get out your high definition, surround sound, virtual reality, video game, and just turn the television on and begin playing war games. Your weapons are your thumbs, your enemy is inside a box, and your position is surrounded by

Doritos, beer and a comfortable couch. Of course, it is all a game because all the firing is making believe and it cannot hurt you.

Now imagine instead of the couch you're in a fighting plane in a space just big enough for your butt, and your arms and your legs fit the allotted area space. The only movement allowed is your two thumbs. Now imagine that the screen in front of you is shooting real bullets. Bullets that can put a hole in your head and you can only shoot back from the position you're in. You've got very little wiggle room, so I guess the bullets can hit you anywhere like arms, legs, or even your left eye. How are you feeling now? You're probably freezing because the climate in the house has reached 60 degrees below zero and the enemy can move about.

That is how tight it was for Abbot Johnson, a sixteen-year-old who went butt end backward into a Wellington tail gunner's slot. He had his two thumbs to fire back at enemy planes heading toward his position. He was not playing a video opponent. He was firing at German fighter planes. At his working altitude it was about fifty to sixty degrees below zero. It was dangerously cold, with no one to talk to, no hot coffee, and no place to relieve himself. If that was the case, and if it really was a problem, and if there is a malfunction in the suit then his urine would freeze. He would be in that position for some time. Could be up to eight hours. Freezing, hungry, alone, shooting at enemy planes with frozen genitals.

Do you think you could do it, at fifteen, in a Wellington being shot at from all directions? Do you think you could be an Abbott Johnson?

Just asking.

He said, "Every day, we would wake early and would eat breakfast, which could always be our last meal. We would go to briefing, and then we would report to our position on the plane, sitting anxiously waiting for the signal for takeoff. We knew it was a one in four chances of anyone completing all assigned missions. We made forty-four missions and we all came back, and yes, I am bragging.

"We were in the sky and searching for enemy targets. Our targets would be oil refineries, railroad tracks, military bases, or shipping docks. As we entered enemy air space we began getting hit with, not only fire from enemy fighter planes, but flak was also coming at us. Flak, originated from ground artillery fire (canon). Flak crews were really good at figuring how high we were and how fast we were going. The projectile was made up of an explosive device which could knock us out of the sky with a direct hit. We did forty-four missions in all and our whole team returned. intact. Not to brag, but we were a damn good team. Changed my mind, I think I will brag. We were one damn good team."

Something not many civilians know was that the Canadian planes were made of linen cloth covered with a thick layer of lacquer over a metal frame.

Abby went on to say, "When our mission was complete, I would look back at all the destruction, knowing we were doing our job but still thinking of any civilians that were killed or wounded and that thought stays with me. It stays with me today. It never leaves. I remember when starting out I made many friends but they kept dying so I stopped making friends. When I look at my wife, my children and my grandchildren I know I did the right thing and I am glad I did my part in stopping Hitler."

What gave this young kid of fifteen the courage, guts and the wherewithal to sit backward in a Wellington and take on the German fighters in the role of the tail gunner? I asked Abby that question and he replied, "I had God, luck, fate, and humor and I guess that did the job." Second question: Why did you join? And he said, "It was the right thing to do, besides beating my brother into the war was a challenge". He laughed. I shut the tape recorder off.

## Questions

1. What was the reason for this war?
   "We were attacked at Pearl Harbor so we had to stop the Japs, and then Hitler declared war on us so they became part of the mix. Lately I think we do the best we can but some time we blow it a lot. We should have finished Desert Storm but politics got in the way. It was harder for the Vietnam vets because a lot of their enemy did not wear uniforms. Those kids really had it tough. It's all politics."

2. What was the role of the black soldier?
"I heard stories about treatment of the black soldier, but I was pretty tied up with my crew and never really dealt with that issue. I heard good and bad stories. We did have black pilots escort us at times to our destination or as far as their fuel could take them. Those pilots were pretty good and they never left our side. They always got us home safe."
3. What was the role of women?
"We could not have done all we did without the support of women at home, in the factories, and nurses who were on the front lines saving lives."
4. What was the role of gays and lesbians?
"Don't ask-don't tell. I really didn't care one way or the other. If they wanted to join and fight for their country let them."
5. What was the role of Native American Indians?
"Never met any but heard some of them were in the pacific and they had developed a code that the Japs couldn't break."
6. What was the role of the media?
no answer
7. What is post-traumatic stress disorder?
"I believe I was lucky. I was lucky because I had an extended family. I went right back to my family, to carpentry, to getting married and raising a family alone."
8. What would you tell young people today about joining the service?
"I think all young people should join the service. I believe that you become strong and independent. They can learn to appreciate their country. But I do remember telling my son Scott that he should enlist. She (pointing to his wife Muriel) said no. He went and it was me who was the nervous wreck."
9. Would you do it again
"Yes, I think I did the right thing, but as I mentioned you do think about it and it never leaves you."

# CHAPTER 9

## *"The Fifty Bucks Guy" Robert Speers - Heritage German - Paratrooper*

### Life Before the War

I had the pleasure of meeting this ninety-two-year-old fellow, and he told me the story of how fifty bucks changed his life, and destined him to become a paratrooper.

He said, "It was so much steadier and slower back when I was a kid."

I could truly imagine him, as he spoke of his youth, as a bushy haired boy running around with the wind blowing at his back and the sun shining down on him. He said, "It was enjoying the freedom of the summer spaces that only farmland can give, that made me so happy."

In spite of the fact that there was no indoor plumbing, the outhouse was 100 feet from the backdoor, and weekly bathing was done in a galvanized tub in the middle of the old kitchen floor, "I would never change it. I enjoyed the freedom of open land and simple living, too much."

When asked how he received the world news he said, "We got most of our news and entertainment on the radio. We would listen to Amos and Andy and the Life of Riley. They were both comedians. Once in a while we would go to the picture show and see heroes like Tom Mix, and Tarzan, for ten cents. Then I would go home and play heroes with my friends."

## Life During the War

Robert Speers no longer had to daydream about being a hero. Due to the attack on Pearl Harbor, and the beginning of WWII, Bob, became a full-fledged grownup overnight.

He went to join the Navy and, "After spending three days on written exams, physical exams, and getting dizzy while taking an eye exam, I was rejected. I stood outside the office, hands in my pockets, head down. I was so frustrated and to top it all off I did not have a plan B."

But as he left the building, he saw this large colorful cardboard poster. He said, "It was showing a picture of a very handsome debonair, tough looking 'John Wayne' type of paratrooper with the message: 'fifty bucks more if you can jump.' So, I joined." Bob became the real handsome debonair tough looking paratrooper. So, it begins, the boy becomes a man and the war invites him to join.

Bob said, "The next I remember I was hearing 'double time, move, move, move'. Our first meal was tomato soup and a fist full of bread. Food got better after that. The rest of the time was a forty-mile hike, with our equipment weighing more than 40 lbs. attached to our backs, and double time, double time, along with twenty-five pushups and then off to special training. Special training was: just jump jump! out of a plane, night and day till we got it right."

He said, "It was time, so we put on our uniforms, climbed aboard and something I had never done before, was sit, just sit, and wait. It was then that I began to wonder what the heck am I doing here. The plane climbed so high I thought we might pass heaven. I gathered my wits, crossed my fingers and hoped I remembered the routine. Then I hear it, 'ready jump.' We jump right over Europe. I'm praying and hoping my chute opens as I go for a safe landing. I had a perfect five jumps during training. So, why am I worried?

"Maybe because, this time, the enemy is shooting at me. The anxiety was building, each of us with our own thoughts, and fears. We knew now that we jumped, we were on our own. Really on our own with the wind, the dark and our God to guide us. We were sitting targets. The moon was shining to 'beat the band' and we could see each other silhouetted as we floated down, which meant enemy on the ground could see the same. If the enemy saw us it would be like sitting duck at a carnival. I barely had my toes to the ground when machine guns began firing at me. I quickly rolled over on my back. with my spine pressed as deeply as possible into the ground I pulled my knife out of its sheath, cut myself out of the chute and crawled to a hedgerow." Bob had no idea where he was but knew wherever it was, he wasn't welcome. So, through the night he crawled for what seemed to be hours. He said, "I knew at any minute I could be dead. I was afraid to use my clicker in case the enemy was near. I crawled through the night, sweaty, scared, and ready for whatever comes. (The clicker was the tool used to identify themselves) It seemed to be a lifetime in war time, but in clock time it was only about six or seven hours that I crawled on my belly, listening for footsteps in the night, feeling for bugs crawling on me, to the thoughts of enemy finding me before I find my guys. It was just about eight hours when I finally met up with five or six of the troopers that had joined together." Bob said, "Not my buddy Chuck though, didn't see him, he was murdered."

Bob stopped, and for a moment seemed to fade back in time. He said "Remember I mentioned my buddy, Chuck. Well, as we were jumping out over Normandy, he didn't even get the chance to release his parachute before they killed him. He was murdered while still in the air. That young fellow who had just begun shaving, was just gone, dead."

Bob soon became one tough son of a gun paratrooper who, with a pat on his butt and a little push, jumped out of a plane and parachuted, in darkness, into enemy lands and fought until the end of WWII.

I wonder if he was thinking of the fifty bucks for jumping or just dealing with the gut-wrenching determination it took to do his job, at the tender old age of twenty. What do you think?

Just asking

## Questions

1. What is the reason for war?
   "I have no one answer - we are at war now and it appears to me that we are on the verge of another WW with the rise of ISIS in the Middle East and the threat of radical Islamists to establish a World Caliphate with Sharia Law. My best explanation for wars can be explained with two words: power and religion."
2. What was the role of the black soldier?
   "I had no contact with black troops except with some truck drivers."
3. What was the role of women?
   "Well, in my opinion, women in the service is like this. They have a place but not in the foxhole with guys. It will lower the standard for all branches. What would happen to her? The position she is put in would be very dangerous. If they are not respected in other countries how do you think they will be treated by the enemy. Then the question of physical abilities during combat. Do you really want your daughter in combat, in a foxhole, surrounded by enemy? I would not want my son in danger, let alone my daughter."
4. What was the role of gays and lesbians?
   "Don't ask-don't tell was the rule of the day. All I know is we had a Chief who was gay and I didn't know about it at the time. He did a great job. Never had any problems with me and so I think if you don't know about it, why push, who cares. He can keep doing a great job as far as I am concerned."
5. What was the role of Native American Indians?
   "The only Indian I knew was Stan Nordwall who was a Lakota Indian we called him Chief. I am aware of the fact that Indians served well in communications in the Pacific as the Japanese were unable to interpret their messages in the Indian language."

# CHAPTER 10

## *"The Silenced Hero" Robert Noble Sr. - Heritage Irish-Army*

What a funny looking boy! The tall scrawny kid with the big ears. That is exactly what Gloria said when she first saw him. She did not know he was the same Robert Noble that she had heard about and that he was the missing in action fellow that she had heard about. She had joined others in praying for him during Novenas at the Catholic Church. She was a little dynamite and went on to marry the tall scrawny guy who, at the old age of nineteen, had just returned from a POW camp in Germany.

### Life Before the War

Robert had no problem joining the service at seventeen since he said, "I felt I was all grown up due to the fact that I was driving a truck at 11 and moving furniture when I was 12, and working fulltime for my dad during the summer, and after school, and week-ends." He continues with, "I was the oldest child of three, not only in my family but the oldest in the whole neighborhood, with only grownups around me like my mother, father, grandmother, grandfather, aunts and uncles, along with two teachers that lived on the second floor of our Dorchester home." Robert had no problem maturing quickly. He tells me, "I never did much wrong since I had so many adults telling me the right thing to do and no one my age telling me different. I was just a quiet kid that did what I was told, did not answer back and respected my elders. Joining the service wasn't that much different. You did what you were told, you did not talk back and had great respect for your drill sergeant. I thought at seventeen it was the right thing to do and believed I could handle it, so I joined."

## Life During the War

"I passed all tests for air corps, for navigator and pilot, but as soon as I was ready to fly a message came down the line. The message was, 'No need for airmen at this time. Those that started in the army should be transferred back to foot soldiers.' So, grunt it is, and no flying in the cards for Robert.

"Well, as far as boot camp went it seemed pretty rough hiking twenty miles with all gear intact, jumping up for drills, and saying yes sir, yes sir and yes sir which usually ended with someone giving fifty pushups. Then the real tests began and we realized what tough really meant. We were commanded to drop on our bellies since the next maneuver would be working our way under a barbed wire course with live ammunition coming right at us."

I believe they knew this training would eventually help them survive but at the instant if it were me, I would be thinking Holy Mother of God I hope friendly fire doesn't hurt.

What do you think? Just asking.

Robert continued, "I completed training and ended up on the Queen Elizabeth heading toward the war, along with 15,000 other troops. Our entire division went across the Atlantic without escort. The waves were gigantic, especially for the grunts whose stomachs had never been on a roller coaster ride or had never been to sea.

"It was impossible to disembark, due to high seas and enormous waves. We had to wait five to six day before we could even try. The waves were having a war of their own as they tossed, battered and flung the disembarking craft to the wind. Finally, the orders are given and with seventy pounds of weight on our back, and slippery netting to maneuver, we grunts work our way down onto the metal craft. The craft was not very stationary and was about a forty-foot drop. If they lost their grip on the net, it was 'Sorry Mate-Too Late.'"

Bob says, "We finally land on solid ground and now hopefully my training kicks in. We dig a hole, jump in, grab our weapon, and wait in silence, in the dark. We are ready to meet the enemy, and it will not be long. It was pitch black, the wind was howling, it was freezing cold and that is when I heard the noise. It was a guttery low sound that I had never heard before, and it was getting closer. When it was upon me, I understood. It was a language; it was the German language."

At the old age of eighteen he steadied his rifle, with hands almost too numb to move, into the firing position. He said "I was ready to shoot; I had my rifle aimed ready to pull the trigger. I stopped, for some reason I just stopped. Something told me wait. You make a decision, you don't know why, and you do not know the consequences of the why, but I lowered my weapon.

If I had shot it would have been an American soldier that died. The Germans were using the captives as shields. It was sixth sense or something."

Robert did not shoot his fellow soldier and that was the beginning of his imprisonment. At the age of eighteen, his long journey of prisoner, pain, torture, and misery began. Before even reaching the prison camp the pain and misery began. Robert said, "The first night of our capture we slept in freezing weather, we had no blankets, we had no heat, and the missing boards on the floor contributed to the noises the wind made as it shot up from under us until we were numb. Then there was the introduction of the little black loaf of bread. It was one loaf to share among four prisoners. It was the meal for the day. In the future the bread became shared by eight."

After eating their quarter of black German bread Robert said, "Myself and other prisoners were forced into a boxcar where they stood in place since there was not enough room to even move. We were given little or no food. I learned a long time ago to take what comes and deal the best I can with it, and that is what I did. I believe that thinking is what kept me alive"

Robert, took a break. You could see the emotions he still felt by that experience just by looking at his facial expressions and into his eyes. I asked if we should take a break, he said no and continued with, "Time in the prison camp gave me time to learn how to swing a pick ax into frozen ground with my bare hands until they could not feel, getting my feet frostbitten due to lack of foot gear, to lose all my weight except for one hundred pounds that barely covered my six-plus height, along with memories that I will never forget." Hanging on to his belief of, take what comes and deal with it is what Robert stated… "is probably what kept me alive."

Bob said, "Once we were settled in camp we were forced to an open field near the camp. It was there that we were forced to work morning to night to dig an anti-aircraft emplacement. We are out in the open and all of a sudden U.S. Air Corps P-47 came in sight to bomb the work we are doing. Not knowing we were prisoners, they pulled up, they headed across the field towards us. We saw what was happening. We were in the middle of a duck hunt and we are the ducks. We run like crazy and dove under any cover we could find. Our guys began strafing us as we ran. We were darn lucky there were no casualties. Two seconds later, like nothing happened, we were told with rifles pointed at us 'get to work' so we just got up and began digging deeper trenches."

Robert celebrated his nineteenth birthday sharing a loaf of bread with eight of his fellow prisoners. He said, "Germans thought they were following the Geneva Convention in treatment of prisoners of war. That was because they saw nothing wrong about sanitary conditions, starvation, medical care, freezing to death, or working to death, they only saw the importance of the loaf of little black bread. When the war turned and Germany could see the end was near, Hitler ordered the killing of all of us prisoners of war. Due to ignoring that order, by many of the camp leaders, over 92,820 Prisoners of Germany lived to tell their story." Robert G. Noble Sr. was one of them.

## Life After the War

He returned home with instructions to keep his mouth shut, lip zipped, or no response as far as what he endured, how he was treated, and how he survived. He was told by his country not to talk about his experience for security reasons. He was left with an eternal feeling of guilt with no place to share it, or leave it. When some of the feedback of the day was, "so you just sat it out, why didn't you try to escape, why didn't you fight" Robert gave no answers. It takes a very strong character to hold your tongue when you know those that are asking questions have no idea of what war is all about.

It was not until 1980 that Bob came to realize he did his job. He joined at seventeen, was captured and became a POW by the age of eighteen, and on his nineteenth birthday he was sharing a loaf of dark bread with eight other prisoners of war on their way to hell.

If those who criticized had been there, I wonder how well they would have fared. What is it that we, as humans, do wrong that make a young man turn old in just three years? To think for a moment that he should feel guilt for being captured and tortured in a POW camp. To make him feel he should never talk about the brutality that he had endured at the hands of the enemy.

What is it that we do as humans? Just asking.

## Questions

1. Why do we have wars?
   "This war was started by the Germans and then the Japanese attacked us."
2. What was the role of the black soldier?
   "Support and transport troops."
3. What was the role of women?
   "There were nurses and sometime in dangerous areas. I do not believe women should enlist except for the role of nurse.".
4. What was the role of native Indians?
   "Guess they were pretty smart. They developed a message system that the Japanese could not break. I believe it was either or both Hopi or Navajo tribes that served in that capacity."

5. What was the role of the media?
"The media covered the activities during WWII well. Some reporters jumped into combat with us. Some like Ernie Pyle. Ernie Pyle was killed in combat.".
6. What was post-traumatic stress disorder in WWII?
"If a person was unable to complete his job and if his senses are all jumbled up and he cannot function to being a detriment to the position, or if he is going to cause grief to my platoon, then it is up to me to decide what to do. There is a breaking point to all of us."
7. What would you tell young people today about joining the service?
"Service is good for our youth. It gives good exercise, a balanced meal, two years of discipline along with independence and self-confidence. It also allows for civic duty by understanding your country, respecting it, and taking care of its environment. They should truly start with the girl/boy scouts. I believe we should all do some form of supporting our country."

# CHAPTER 11

*"My Rights" Erasmo Martinez -Heritage Latino - Navy*

He was sitting outside, with his girlfriend, at the VFW Hall. I was there because I was looking for veterans to interview. He was the perfect veteran to interview. He had a twinkle in his eye that most lose with adult life, and a smile that went right across from one ear to the other. I think he had been waiting for me for a long time because he was ready.

## Life Before the War

I asked if he could tell me a bit about life before the war. He started by sitting up straight, shoulders back and with a sober tone to his voice he said: "My name is Erasmo Martinez and I was born and raised in a little Texas town called La Car. I lived there until I was twelve. I am an American with Mexican heritage. My dad came from Mexico to America when he was seventeen. He got a job, worked hard, bought a farm, married a beautiful Spanish lady, and they had nine children. I was one of the youngest. We all worked the farm picking mostly cotton and corn. My early education consisted of learning strong work ethics, integrity, pride in self and family. I was lucky enough to be born with a little bit of humor and lot of common sense." I think I saw a bit of that humor when I asked Erasmo what his nationality was. He replied "They call us Mexican; they call us Spanish; they call us Mexican /American; they call us Hispanic or Latino," and with a most satirical grin added "along with many, many other names. But today I think you could call me Latino." I wondered what all the other names were that he did not mention. I did not ask. But it was then that I realized that humor was probably a good technique to use for survival.

That humor came out again when asked who was in charge of the family. "My dad was in charge. He was a 'man.' He was my role model. We did exactly what he said because we loved him." Then with a little grin and a little hesitation, "...and because there was no place to run to, and no place to hide. So, we did not disobey." He said, "We would get a birthday gift and a Christmas gift and all else was divided by nine. We did not have things like refrigerators, telephones, or cars. We had two feet and three miles of road to get to town."

It was in1939 when they left the farm. Erasmo said, "When we left the farm, I was twelve and I really missed my life there. We moved to Michigan and things changed. It was so cold with little freedom because our days were taken up with 'school.' My dad had home schooled us but because he taught us in Spanish, we needed to start public school in the first grade. No problem, even though I am twelve and all others are about seven years old. I had to start in the first grade but did not stay long. I did all the work for the first six grades in one year and caught up to my age group. One thing I learned was that I knew a lot about life that city kids never got." To be smart enough to skip one grade for any kid at any school was awesome. I asked if he received an award or recognition for doing six in one year. He put on that grin and just said "NOOOO."

## Life During the War

It is 1944, and Erasmo Martinez was just seventeen. He is in his junior year of high school and has just received his draft notice. World War II is ready to introduce Erasmo to the action. With little experience in world travel he is about to enter into a "twilight zone" half way around the world. It is called the Pacific Theater. Okinawa to be exact.

He said, "Twenty of us home-grown guys, around age seventeen, decided we would all go together and join the navy. We all stuck together during the fourteen weeks of training. So far not bad, but then training was over and we were all separated and assigned to different ships. After that we never did get to see each other again. Only nine out of the twenty of us returned home. Adios mi amigos."

He said, "I never did get training for what happened next. It was a complete surprise to me. My head was beating like the large drum that is always at the end of a parade, thump, thump, thump. My stomach was turning like the earth on its axis ever so slowly over, and over, and over, until it had emptied out everything that I had taken in for the last twenty-four hours. On top of that I was dizzy sitting, standing, or even laying down. I was trying to remember why I joined the Navy. Oh ya, I did not want to join the Army and have 'feet on the ground.' I can remember thinking 'right now I would like my feet on ground anywhere but here.' This surprise was called sea sickness which lasted for about three days. Salt tablets, crackers or lemonade was the diet but not the cure. With ten months to go I was praying that this does not happen again.

"At the time of war, we did not receive training except to kill first and ask questions later. My job until enemy approach was as store keeper. Then I became a fighting sailor along with every other sailor on the ship. I was part of the team that was responsible for the firing of the 40mm gun and we were a well-oiled group with one 'pointer' to elevate the gun, two 'trainers' dealt with the horizontal movement of the gun and the remaining four would deal with loading the ammunition. I was one of the four.

"Our job, along with three other destroyers, was to protect the cruisers so they could land safely. The sailors knew 'friendly' Kamikazes would be dropping by, literally dropping by and staying for life." Erasmo said, "We knew that we wanted to survive and return home. We knew that the Japanese flyers did not plan on surviving to return home. Instead they planned on flying their planes at high speed, loaded with bombs, right into our ships to destroy as many sailors and as much equipment as possible. We knew that we had to aim fast, shoot fast and duck fast in order to make it home." Erasmo stopped for a second and then continued in a serious tone. "When in battle we were a family of sailors. We all took care of each other. We knew someone would cover our back and we would cover theirs. There was no discrimination on the ship during the fighting. We needed each other to make it home."

I asked if there was discrimination before he joined. With a grin on his lips but not in his eyes he said "If not being allowed at certain dances, certain schools, certain stores, certain jobs and being segregated from the white population is discrimination then, with a drawn-out grin, he said yessssssssss, there was discrimination." He then went on to say, "I came home from war much older and wiser than the seventeen-year-old- kid who joined. I could speak English and now I knew my rights, and when I had children, they would know theirs."

## Questions

1. *Why do we have wars?*
   No answer.
2. What did you think about women in the service?
   "I don't recall that there were any women serving in the armed forces when I was serving my country. There probably were some women serving in the military at that time, but they might have been at the home front and not at the war front. I do not recall women being recruited into the U.S. armed forces during World War II. There might have been women in the medical field, but I don't know if they were military personnel or civilians. I believe that the men belonged in the war, but I don't believe that women belonged in the war at that time."
3. What did you think of black soldiers during the war?
   "There were only two black soldiers that I knew of or served with during war time on my ship. My ship was a destroyer, the USS Nields 'DD 616'. Their duty was to serve the officers aboard the ship unless it was a war situation or a defensive situation. If that occurred, these men were assigned to their battle positions like anyone else on the ship and they would do that job next to the white men. During my time in the military, race and segregation were very strong in the USA and in the military.

During military training, white men trained separate from black men. I did not see any black men during my time of training as they trained elsewhere (unknown where). It was not until I got to my assignment on my ship that I served with these two black men. During my time in the military, white men and black men did not eat, drink, sleep or socialize together including on the ship. I recall that these things changed sometime around the year 1954 after I was out of the military. I did not appreciate the fact that the black soldiers were discriminated against or segregated from the others even though they were American sailors fighting for their country too."

4. What do you think about Gays and Lesbians in the service?
   "Gays and Lesbians have always existed. Now that they have come out and / or been exposed in the military. I believe that as long as they are Americans and are physically able and are willing to serve our country, I believe it's okay for them to be in the service."
5. Do you think the media is fair when reporting on war issues?
   "So far, the wars that are ongoing today are such a mess that I can't really understand what's going on. On a scale of one to ten, one being the worst, I give the media a six today because I believe that a lot of the war news, we hear today from the media is neither all truth or misinformation. I believe that today's newspapers, television reports, and radio station reports are all about national media ratings."
6. What would you tell young people today about joining the service?
   "Yes, I believe they should in one form or another. When I was in the service, women took over the jobs that men left when they went to war. Others (men and women) volunteered for the USO, medical field and other organizations. These people were helping or serving somehow during war time.

# CHAPTER 12

*"Decoy" Charlie Villa - Heritage Italian-Navy*

## Before the War

At ninety-four, Charlie is still dancing the Jitter Bug, role playing Charlie Chaplin at special occasions and still has a lovely lady on his arm. He still has a great sense of humor and was just honored at Fenway Park, home of the Red Sox baseball team, for his military service.

My first question was, could you please tell a bit about your parents. You could see he was proud about what he was going to say. He sat straight back in his chair, put both hands on the table, and in a very somber tone said, "My dad, James Villa, was strong. In his teen years he went right into the coal mines of Pennsylvania. He worked the jobs of the hardened men that had been there for many years. After leaving the mines he became a boxer. He was pretty good at it. Then, he had to stop because of the bad breathing that caught up with him from the mines. I can't remember what it was called but I know he died at fifty-eight because of it. My dad, he had a calming kind of personality. Back then the mother would wait for the dad to get home to punish the kids. Not in my house. My dad was too easy going with a good sense of humor so he left that job for my mother. I think I got the love of dance from my dad and my sense of humor from him also. Things did not upset him like they did my mom.

My mom, Lina was the one I got punishment from. She kept me in line. If she hadn't, I might have been a bum. I remember one day, God knows I drove her crazy some days, she hit me over the head with a plate. The plate broke, I was fine. So, the next time she tried the broom. I was just one of those kids that got in trouble without even trying. I was lucky I had a very hard head. My mom was also the one that taught me to respect elders, be honest, do well in school and work hard. I had the best of both worlds. My dad was calm and direct with me. My mom was a terrible cook but made me grow up and be responsible. Then I had my grandmother who just loved me for me. She also was the best ever Italian cook in the world."

The next question was where and when did you start working? Charlie looked at me smiled and just started talking. With his very animated Italian gestures, he said, "the whole family picked blueberries until we had gallons collected. Then my second job was to sell door to door for twenty-five cents a quart. I also picked mushrooms, ran errands for change, sold peanuts at the boxing matches for ten cents a bag. Then when I got to be about fifteen, I worked as busboy at a local nightclub. When I wasn't working, me and my friends would play baseball, flirt with the girls, and sometimes skip school. It was a lot of fun until the truant officer caught us at the local movie theater. Then it wasn't fun no more."

I asked Charlie why he joined. His response surprised me. He said "I didn't join. They drafted me two months before I graduated from high school. I was mad. I missed the last of my senior year. The fun, the dance, the graduation, and my mother had to pick up my diploma. I was so mad. When I got there to sign-up, I had a choice army or navy. I had always loved the navy. Remember now, I'm a schmuck who's never been nowhere but my neighborhood and now I am going to who knows where, ya I'm a bit mad and a bit nervous."

## During the War

I asked Charlie if he could tell us about the beginning of his adventure in the Navy. He said, "One story about training, I will tell. You see, you have to be able to swim the length of a pool in order to stay in the Navy. After the second try my instructor said, 'You don't make the next try, you're out. You see, I do not want to go to the Army. Nothing wrong with those guys. It is just, I'm short and the idea of carrying forty pounds on my back, I don't know. So, the only thing to do is cheat. I got my buddy to take my tags, take a test at another time and son-of-a gun I passed. First lucky break of many. I will tell you I did wear a safety vest ninety per cent of the time when I was at sea. My second break came even before stepping on board. You see, my name ended in a V which made me very lucky. The reason being the first ship '426' was filled before they reached my name. I was put on ship '427'. Ship 426 was bombed by the Germans and the men on that ship died. It is luck, we all say it, it is just luck."

What is the next step, I ask? Charlie said, "First job on the Hilary P. Jones (DD427) was to help pass magazines up to gunners. Now, like I said, I was a small guy and now, even though the ship is big I am in a small claustrophobic space. I got to get out of there so, there is a test for a sonar operator. I ask to take the test. For some reason I studied and when it was time to take the test, I found all the answers in the back of the test book. So, I had studied, but to not look at the back page, 'come on' I became a sonar operator. I began tracking the beeps in the ocean and searching for submarines. We detected, and with the help of three escort vessels, attacked U-616 off Algeria and sent it to the bottom. The enemy just blew right out of the water."

But the best story which not many know is we were a decoy for the attack on D-Day. Our mission was to get the Germans to think we were going to attack from the south of France. We set up in Africa. I mean the whole shebang. First, we got the Germans attention. They took the bait and started down toward the south of France. We kind of played with them till they got close and then, 'you wouldn't believe it', we retreated and really blew their minds. It was then, when they decided to turn and go, we hit them. We did electronic jamming to prevent radio- controlled bombs from enemy harassing the area. Planes began dropping bombs and telling us where we should land our gunfire. Well, let me tell you, it was like a fourth of July with all the fireworks. We did our job. We were the decoy and we did our job. I was never so proud to be an American."

We took a break from the war and I asked Charlie about Navy down time? Again, Charlie is using his Italian hand language and his voice.

He says, "I'm going to tell you this story and this story is true. Now, we would have the local whore house guarded so our guys were not allowed in, right, but the French could go in. I waited till a group of them started toward the house and just snuck in. So far so good, but here comes the bad part. Before I get to enjoy myself, the Shore Patrol bangs through the door. They yell 'Americans'! Shit, I'm in trouble. I jump into the littlest closet you would ever see. I tried not to make a sound not even breath, and all I can think about is I am in a closet in a whore house fighting a war. Hey, it's the truth."

## After the War

So, you're discharged and for the first time in your life you have no one ordering you around. What do you do? "First", he says, "I take the fifty-two-twenty offered by the government." He looks at me and says, "you don't understand this and so I'll explain. The government gave us veterans twenty dollars for fifty-two weeks to help get our feet back on the ground. Hey, I took it. Then I met my wife, we dated, got married and I got a job working in my brother-in-law's plastic company and learned every job in the shop so I could go out on my own and start my own business." He stopped my next question by saying, "Wait, I forgot a story. I was selling my plastic wares at a convention. They were all sports trophies like football, basketball, but best of all baseball. You got to see the picture. I am sitting behind the table and I think I am dreaming because walking down the aisle in front of my table, my god, it was Ted Williams, the best ballplayer ever. He shook my hand, he talked to me, he talked to me for over five minutes. Can you believe that, Ted Williams?"

So, now I ask my next question which was about family, and he said, "Hey, I loved my wife, my three kids, dancing, and baseball. I served my country and came home safe. I got to shake the hand of the legend Ted Williams and at ninety-four was just honored for my military service at Fenway Park, the home of the Red Sox baseball team. Life can't get better."

## Questions

1. Why are there wars?
   So, Charlie reminds me again by saying while waving his arms and smiling, "You know I'm ninety - four, so I could make a mistake, but I think we never start a war unless we have to. We have a good way of life and other countries want what we have so we have to keep them down sometime."
2. What was role of black soldiers?
   "They did the basic work like cook and wait on us at meal times."
3. What treatment was there for PTSD.
   "Never heard of that word back then."
4. How were women treated?
   "Most women that I met were nurses." He chuckles and says, "except for the story I told you."
5. How were gays treated?
   "If they were found they would get kicked out. Not so nicely."
6. What was the role of the media?
   "We were on ship so much we never knew anything."
7. Would you do it again?
   "Only if I was sure it would end up the same way. You know dancing, being happy, and living this long."
8. What would you tell young people today about joining?
   "How can I tell them to go. I didn't even want to go." Then Charlie says after a moment, "OK, if it could turn out for them like it did for me, sure join."

# CHAPTER 13

*"Flying Bird"- Flora Bella Reece - Heritage - WASP*

## Life Before the War

I could tell that this is a woman's story that should become familiar to all young girls who have dreams. Her name is Flora Bella, and she had her feet strongly planted on the ground by the age of seven, with a dream. She knew this is what she wanted and she was going for it no matter what barriers lie ahead. This was a dream way before it was acceptable for "ladies" to even think such things. Flora Bella wanted to fly, and she was going to fly.

It wasn't hard to see that she was a no-nonsense person. I knocked on the door, she opened it, she said, "Come in, have seat, I'll pour some coffee and we can begin. So, where would you like to start." I could tell in those first minutes that she did not waste time, so, I took out my recorder and we got right to work.

I told her I would like to start with her childhood. If she could tell me a bit about her background as far as parents, siblings, and environment. Without hesitation she began.

"We lived on a farm until I was in the third grade. My dad was a preacher and a sharecropper. He taught us children to be honest and follow the word of God. I tried to follow, but some time with just a little bit of deviation. It wasn't that I was bad, just didn't know what I was doing wasn't right. It was my father who would get me back on track with just a very quick look. He was very supportive of whatever direction in life his kids wished to go. So, I told him how I had always admired birds just flying in the air, and that I wanted to fly and be a pilot someday. He didn't laugh. He said, 'Flora Bella, that isn't something girls usually do, but if you can figure out a way to make it happen, more power to you.'

"Mom was a homemaker, pianist, and seamstress, and a good mother. Since it was during the depression, she made all our clothes from donations we were given by the church. She would rip them up and re-make them to fit us to a T, without a pattern. When I was graduating from high school I asked for a readymade dress, a real readymade dress. I was seventeen and finally wore a real store-bought dress to graduation. She taught us to care for those less fortunate than ourselves, to be good to all people no matter how different, and to thank God for what we have.

"This was the time of the Great Depression and us kids did thank God and did not complain for work we did, like plow the field with my brother when I was just ten. It never dawned on us to complain, while, maybe just a little, if I recall. We were happy we could eat and there was no better place for children to grow. The healthy freedom we had then, I wish on all children today."

## During the War

I asked if she could tell me how she ended up flying planes for the military. She said, "Just as I was finishing my senior year, the Japanese bombed Pearl Harbor, and WW II for America began. It was at this time I happened on a notice, in the local paper, that a Jacqueline Cochran was looking for women twenty- one years old or older to fly military aircraft for the Army. This is my chance to fly. So, I sent for my birth certificate, even though I was only seventeen and knowing I would have to wait a few years because of my age. But, by luck they sent me my older sister's certificate which made me nineteen and so with a little white lie I'm in. I was excited to meet her. She was a WASP (Women Air Service Pilot). Cochran was one of the women who broke the barrier for women to fly." Talk about breaking a glass ceiling.

Flora Bella went on to say, "I went for the interview. I was elated and could not contain myself when I passed the interview and the physical.

Then the shoe dropped. I was told I would need to pay for thirty-five hours of flying time in order to join the W.A.S.P. It was like asking me for the moon. But God bless my brother, he stepped up and paid without ever questioning me. This moment is what I had dreamed of my whole life. I was to fly and at the same time serve my country."

I asked what the first step to entering the WASP was. She replied, "We entered training dressed like young ladies and in no time at all we were dressed in oversized jumpsuits. Some suits fit, some were too big, some too small and I for one didn't even care. I was going to fly. I was so ready." She just smiled and said, "Did you know that I learned to fly a plane before I learned to drive a car and I was only seventeen." At times she was so animated that I really believed she was re-living those moments. She said, "Our quarters were a little tight, but we survived. We came together with different religions, financial backgrounds and dreams and we made it work. We were sisters in the air.

My training took place in Clearwater, Texas, and we settled into a tremendously hot, hot summer with a very cold winter to follow. We were pretty much alone except for the little creatures that crawled in the day and night, like snakes and other little squirmy things.

It was about six weeks into training and my Catholic background got to me, so I had to tell my age even though the average age was twenty-one and I went in as nineteen but was really only seventeen. When I look back, I realize how very young I was. I went and told my commander with my fingers crossed. He said, the age limit is being lowered and you are doing a good job so just do it. I knew then that God was watching me and kind of giving the OK for me to fly.

I was trained to fly the Vultee B-13, Stearman PT-17, the American AT-16 and the Martin B-26, performing military missions state wide. One of my duties was to fly towed targets for gunnery practice with a Martin B-26 Marauder. Gunnery practice was that I would carry a dummy target attached to the tail of my plane and then the artillery trainees below would practice shooting the dummy, which as I said, is attached to the end of my tail. I did wonder a bit about that particular duty, especially when it was said WASPs were never in any danger. I just hoped they knew I was not the dummy."

I would like to inject a short statement to back Flora Bella's comment about the danger of the target artillery training. A sailor, by the name of Stacky Nicas told me while he was practicing shooting as an artillery trainee, he almost shot the tale of the plane that was carrying the dummy target. He said "Couldn't believe I did that. We were just practicing. I positioned my weapon to fire and I hit the wire holding the dummy. I couldn't believe it. I hit it within inches of the tail of the plane. I'm not that good of a shot. Accidents happen, and I was so glad it only hit close. Glad, I didn't shoot one of our planes down."

Just a side bit of info, the name of the plane that Flora Bella flew was also known as the Widow Maker. So, what do you think so far, any danger there? Just asking.

She continued by saying, "Another responsibility we had was to check the planes that came back for repairs. We would do this by taking them up, and try them to see if they stayed up.", She said "We were in danger and we still stood strong." Again, do you think they were in danger? Just asking.

She said, "One thing we could do that the male pilots could not was say no to our commanding officer. But, if we did, Jacqueline Cochran who developed the program would simply send you packing. Did you know she was the first woman to break the sound barrier? She was tough on us because she knew we were breaking barriers of our own.

I just want to say that the statement 'women were never in any danger' was wrong. Thirty-eight of my fellow WASPs died. When one of our 'fly girls' died, and since we were not recognized as military service, we would have to take a collection of our own to send the body home for burial. There were no honors, no medals, and no flag was placed on their coffin.

Discharge day was in December, 1944 we were disbanded. We were not recognized for our contributions. I think we should have at least gotten a thank you when they told us our job was done and we could get ourselves home. It took seventy years for us to be awarded the Congressional Gold Medal and I tell you right now I would happily give that medal back if I could have gotten more time flying.

"What I have told you is my truth. But, even with all the discrimination, I still would do it again. I did my part to serve and I did it flying. I hope the younger generations know that WASPs are the reason why women are flying in the service today. Hope they keep breaking barriers."

## After the War

I looked at this small-framed woman with short curling hair, a twinkle still in her eyes, and wonder what have I done to compare to this beautiful woman's life. Before I could continue further into my own thoughts she interrupts with, "As you can see I 'm not in a rocking chair yet." So, I ask 'what's next' as I'm thinking she would say a quiet life, family, homebody. Nope, I was wrong.

Flora Bella begins, "I married my first love who I went to high school with. We had three children and we lived in California."

I asked what married life was like. She replied, "I was lucky. I had a forward-thinking man and having his wife working outside the house was not a problem. He also understood my need for education, and so I went to school and received my papers to become a teacher." So, were you teaching aviation? "No" was the reply, "but I was teaching math and was one of the first teachers that encouraged and initiated the first Apple II computer lab. It was hard because at the time teachers thought that computers were a passing fancy."

So, did you ever retire? Her answer was, "No, when I left teaching, my husband and I went with our church and spent two years in the Peace Corps in Malaysia, Thailand and India." She looks at me, and giving that genuine down to earth smile of hers, said, "Don't ever retire or stop growing, life is a treasure, don't waste it."

She was proof of her statement because she was still volunteering in the Philippines in 2009, and continued to show slides of her experience while in the WASP to many schools and other organizations.

It is women like Flora Bella, a barrier breaker, that make you wonder 'what have you done to make a difference?" Her words to me were, "Don't sit too long and always have a direction." I asked her what was her life direction and she said "God first, family second and flying third that was my direction, young people need to find theirs." I did not have the opportunity for a second interview because this amazing woman died before that could happen.

## Questions

1. Why are there wars?
   "I personally feel that as Americans we must fight for every individual in the world. We must back Israel, it is the only democratic country in the area. It aggravates me the way Obama is treating them, they are God's chosen people.
   "I also believe that some wars do not have to be fought, like Vietnam, and if they are going to go to war, then they should give the military the authority to take care of it instead of politically pussy footing around and then leaving them in there."
2. What was the role of black soldiers?
   "I know there was segregation between black and white so it follows that would be the same in the service. I always felt that we were all children of God."
3. How were women treated?
   "We were not seen as equal to men but, did you know, that despite that we had women spies as field operatives and thousands more were members of the OSS which was the beginning of the CIA."
4. How were gays treated in the service?
   "It was keeping your mouth shut and tell no one. It was so complicated. No one would want to undress. It is so sick and complicated."
5. What was the role of the media?'
   "In WWII, there was radio, newspaper, and word of mouth and everyone knew what was going on, even the young. There was an article in the Herald American that gave credit for what we were doing. I was proud that we were being recognized. I wish they still had the Christian Monitor."
6. What would you tell young people today about joining?

"I would remind them of what President Kennedy said, 'Ask not what your country can do for you, but what you can do for your country.' I feel bad for some young people. No one cares enough to be strict with them, discipline them, and help them grow and become responsible adults."

7. Would you do it again?

   "I wish I was still flying, and yes, I would do it again."

# CHAPTER 14

## *"Red Tail" Granville C Coggs Heritage-Black American- Air Force*

It was not planned. It was not expected, but as veterans have told me throughout their stories it is luck, just pure luck that things happen and that is exactly how it happened that I met this amazing "Red Tail" pilot.

You see, my husband Charlie, who is a retired air force major, was showing me the T-38 that he had flown. We were at Randolph Air Force Base in San Antonio Texas, where he had trained and that is where we learned there was a Tuskegee Airman about to give a speech.

We entered the building, and I requested direction to Dr Coggs. He sat with shoulders back, feet outstretched, and his expression, when I approached, was relaxed and inviting. So, saying something about the very colorful hat he had on did not cause me any distress. He smiled and asked what he could do for me. When I explained my purpose and requested an interview, not meaning that moment, he said three minutes you got three minutes. I, being the great interviewer that I was, went completely blank and just looked at the very distinguished Dr. Granville C Coggs, MD and Red Tail WWII veteran. After about a minute of silence, thank you for your service and my freedom was about all I could say. He smiled and I left. Strike one on me for not being the best interviewer in the world. Took about a five-hour plane trip home while beating myself up to decide on strike two. I wrote a letter requesting a do-over of those three minutes and believe it or not that gentleman wrote back and said if you're willing to pay plane fare to just come see me I certainly have time to see you.

Charlie and I flew back to Texas and in a more informal luncheon with himself and his wife Maude I had my interview. He began by calling us his new friends and invited us into the living room.

As I always do, first question, can you tell me about your family and your childhood.

"We can start with my name Granville. It was the name of a slave, my great grandfather. So, from the very beginning hard work, great expectations and humility were in order. Humility came first. At the age of seven I was given the job of emptying the slop jars every morning before going to school since there was no in-door plumbing. Great expectations came when I was about ten years old and I saw a movie titled "West Point" of the air and it showed all white pilots, which gave me the understanding that blacks could not be pilots. It did not take long for my parents to set me straight. I was told that just because there are some who hold the erroneous racial stereotype that blacks did not have the intellectual capacity to learn to fly doesn't mean you can't. Expect a lot of yourself, work hard and with God all things are possible. My parents always encouraged us to excel, but that was not always the case outside. I remember the time I went to a white school to take the SAT exam and when I asked the white tester where should I sit? Since it was still during segregation in America with the Jim Crow attitude flying high, his statement was, 'sit anywhere you want, you ain't going to pass anyway.' When I received the results, my score was higher than any other test taker in the room, guess the instructor was wrong."

Looks like the tester tested wrong. What do you think? Just asking

## During the War

With the support of his parents and with the understanding, at a very young age, that a black kid has to do twice as good as a white kid to succeed in the world, Granville Goggs started his travels into the WWII arena.

I asked why did he join, and he explained that he felt that his turn for the draft was knocking on the front door and he decided to beat it to the punch.

He said, "Instead of ending up in the infantry I would have the option of volunteering for the Black Army Air Corps. I knew that would give me the opportunity for blacks with talent or capability to, instead of infantry, to possibly be a flyer, an officer, and a respected individual. Remember I told you about seeing the movie where there were no black pilots and remember I told you my parents said if you think you can, you can. Well, guess they were right. I am training to be a Tuskegee Red Tail. I am going to be a black pilot, and I am starting my training at the young age of seventeen."

Would you tell a little bit about your initial training? He said, "I began my training in December of forty-three. I received by private status, picked up my uniform, and began basic training. I remember little about basic except coming from my family's belief that if a job was given to you then you do it. I did it. What I do remember is that I never left the base. It was in the middle of segregated black Mississippi and you did not want to find out what white Mississippians might do." This period of time in our history the Green Book and the Jim Crow rules were still very active.

"My next step was training as a bombardier. My position would be that of auxiliary gunner and my responsibility would be to ensure that the plane was not attacked by the enemy while flying to the target. But before I could become a bombardier, I would need to learn the skills of the gunner. After receiving my gunner badge, I returned for my training as a bombardier. I graduated as a Bombardier in 1945."

Thinking of all Dr Coggs had told me about his life and how he had learned 'if you want it you can get it', I decided to ask how it felt to get it. I was thinking he must be so happy to succeed this far. His answer was "it was bitter sweet. I did graduate, that was sweet. but when the pictures of all the graduating cadets were printed in the hometown newspapers, mine was left out. The reason, 'It is simply our policy not to print pictures of colored in our newspaper.'

So, now that you have accomplished something that you thought in childhood could never happen, becoming a pilot, what next? "Yes, I became a pilot but a black one and blacks were not sent into war because the Air Force didn't want anything to do with black pilots; therefore, the pilots were sent directly to train in North Africa. Due to their many military successes the Army decided to use them to protect the bombers that were dropping bombs over Berlin. These are the guys who painted the tail of their planes with red paint, so the name Red Tails became known.

I asked Dr. Coggs if he could tell me the successes of the Red Tail. This was a question I could tell he was pleased with. He began with, "Did you know that The Tuskegee Airmen were totally segregated from the main stream of the military. They flew many missions for our country and were very successful in destroying German fighter jets and a German destroyer along with protecting our bombers so they would reach their goal. Many of these men who were fighting against the Axis power and at the same time against discrimination. If my memory serves me the numbers were about three-hundred served as pilots, at least 150 Flying Crosses were earned and they destroyed over 250 enemy planes." Although the war did not wait until Granville completed his training as a Red Tail he said, "I still take great pride in the fact that I did complete the requirements and was ready to go. I just listened to my parents, who I was lucky to be born to, when they said, 'It is what you think of yourself not what others think of you.' These words really helped me this far on my life's path.

When I was discharged my direction was clear I married my sweetheart Maud, and we began attending the University of Nebraska. We rented a small room outside the university due to the fact that they did not allow blacks to live in the dorms or eat in the cafeteria. My wife graduated with a bachelor's in chemistry, along with a master's degree. I was top three in my class and elected Phi Beta Kappa, Sigma Xi, and Phi Lambda Upsilon honor societies." I told him I thought bragging rights were in order. He wasn't finished. Granville went on to become a doctor, established the first ultrasound division at UC San Francisco, invented the "Central X-ray beam Guided Breast Biopsy System" and just to top it off he became a senior runner in track and field competition with six gold medals to his name.

They did allow the black students to pay the same tuition as others just not with the same benefits. What do you think?

Just asking.

Granville said, "Can you believe that I have lived long enough to go from fear of walking down a Mississippi street simply because I am black, to seeing a black man become president of the United States." Granville said, "at the age of seven I was emptying slop due to no indoor plumbing to becoming a Red Tail, a doctor, an inventor and being invited with my daughter to President Obama's inauguration. I would never have believed that this day could happen."

I think that Granville has put to rest the notion of a brain size. I believe there are many cultural brains out there that would not dare compete with Granville's.

What do you think?

Just asking

## Questions

I did not have the opportunity to return a third time to finish our interview therefore I am left with any empty space for answers.

So, I would like to just share a few thoughts in this empty space. After listening to Dr. Coggs, and reading his book "Soaring Inspiration" I believe the reason young black men joined the service was to show that they were physically, emotionally and intellectually equal to all others who joined. That the courage, they would demonstrate in battle would support, on returning home, equality for equal levels of opportunity in the work, living, and education fields.

When the war was over President Truman decided to begin the desegregation of the military. Granville said he believed it to be in part due the superior job of the Red Tails. Desegregation in the military was the first step. The second step took much longer. The Jim Crow Laws that Granville has mentioned, along with the Green Book took about thirty plus years to disband.

## New Weapons Used in WWII

The weapons that the world had previously used in WWI seemed "not-up-to-snuff", a term old timers used to mean not sufficient enough to do the job, so during this war, as in every previous conflict, it was decided new and more modern weapons were needed such as:

**The Thompson Submachine gun** A man by the name of John Thompson envisioned a gun that could act like a trench broom and with just one sweep through a dugout would annihilate the enemy in just seconds. This gun was first named "the Annihilator" or the "Persuader" because of the quick and deadly carnage it could inflict, but later was given the name of the inventor, "Thompson Submachine gun". It was the favorite of many foot soldiers during WWII because it was able to, with just one sweep of their arm, clear out one entire trench

**Mk II Grenade** This grenade was also called a "pineapple" due to its shape and appearance. It could be thrown about 30 yards. Although it had the shortest range in terms of 'throwing distance' it was still preferred due to the extremely forceful effect it had on its target. Its power could annihilate a room of enemy troops in seconds.

**Sherman Tank** This tank was fast, cheap, and dependable and since it was believed superior to the German Panzer III and IV, America thought this weapon (the Sherman Tank) could win the war. They believed it so strongly that they put no further pressure on tank development

**Communication** Citizens still received information via radio, movies, newspapers and word of mouth. Throughout WWII some of its military methods of communication were still expedited by foot, motorcycle, automobile and/or airplane. Code talkers, who were the Native American Navajo Indians, transformed their native language into a code that the Japs could not decipher. One of the technical developments of WWII was the electronic computers, such as battlefield equations, ballistics, and more. Numerous small digital computers which were used on the battle field helped the ships to shore hit targets more precisely. The computer which was primarily used for breaking the "Enigma", which was the Nazi's secret codes, was developed by Alan Turing who was a war hero and computer pioneer. He was also a gay man who was treated bad, terribly bad by his government.

Do you know what happened to this hero? Just asking.

## Letter Home

### A Soldier's Letters Home: November 24, 1944

Dear Mother & Dad,

I received my first letters from you yesterday since I've been overseas. There were three of them, 2 v-mail and 1 airmail. I'm glad you finally sent me Rum's address. Now I will be able to write to him.

Yesterday was Thanksgiving. We had the turkey and all the trimmings. Most of the doughboys had turkey also. It's amazing when you think of all of us, so far from home, observing still in the midst of a battlefield, Thanksgiving. I'm sure there was many who gave thanks to God today. I was sure one of them.

I recently was able to see some of the dead boys they had just taken off the battlefield. If some of the men back home, whom of personal ambition attempt to prolong the war, could see them--I'm sure the war would soon end. When you look at them you can't help but think--why are they dead! Just a year or so ago they were either going to school-working-married and now their dead. Many among them had ambition--all looked forward to the future--Now their dead. It keeps shooting thru your mind-again and again-why have these men died? I know why we fight-I know of the values we're trying to secure. I hope these men have not given their lives for empty words.

I'm sorry I went up on slight a philosophical side. But I had to air out some of my thoughts. Love, Harold

# KOREAN WAR

**Voice of Humanity –**
**The Chosin Place, A poem**

Korea, bloodshed, land and mountains
Have been bathed by youthful fountains.
Brave men here have gone to their reward
Perishing 'neath the sword.
Korea, twas not a war they say;
Only a police action day by day,
A testing place
For the human race.
Korea, two ideals clashing
Communism and democracy smashing;

*The poem is by S/SGT Irvin V. Worden, on 14 December 1953, while stationed in Korea.*

# AS THEY REMEMBER

# CHAPTER 15

*American Life in the Fifties*

It is five years after WWII and the people of white suburban America have settled down to the music of Perry Como, Nat King Cole, and Pattie Page; of children taking their well-earned nickels to the local movie theater to watch the daily newsreel that always came on just before cartoons like Bugs Bunny and Donald Duck. Those cartoons would fill kids with humongous belly laughs and leave them with hyped-up happiness for the day. There was always a Sunday dinner at gramma's house with all the children dressed in church-going outfits. Little girls had fluffy dresses and little hats and gloves. Boys had suits with 'white shirt and tie' or little sailor suits. The games of the time were marbles, Olly Olly in-Free, baseball, bike riding and Kick the Can.

Few families had televisions and so the weekly theater newsreel along with the daily newspaper and radio news updates, were the avenue for information on the world. At that time the local papers would give pretty much the community information with, occasionally, an update on the world news, ergo the Forgotten War.

## The Korean War/ The Forgotten War

War by any other name is still a war. It is not a "police action," which was the term that President Truman used to address the crisis that was smoldering in Korea. Truman felt the American people were not ready to hear the word "war" since they had, just a few years back, been in a world war and were trying to pull themselves back to normalcy. That term was quickly changed to "war" by the United Nations.

There was no doubt in the minds of the troops that were sent over to Korea that it was war. Just ask any veteran who happened to be there. They were shot at, they were wounded, they were frozen, they were crippled and maimed, and some never came home. It was war, and this war started long before North Korea invaded South Korea. It started with the birth of the Cold War. Its main purpose was called containment. Due to the strong differences in ideology between the two super powers that emerged after WWII, which were the Soviet Union who believed in communism, and America who believed in capitalism/democracy, this new war began. Both superpowers wanted their idealism to spread throughout the world. It was called the "Domino Theory" which the U.S. belief was that if one country was forced into communism then a series of other countries would fall like a line of dominoes.

A small country, half way around the globe, called Korea, would be the battle ground. When the Japanese were defeated by the allies in WWII, they lost control of Korea. The Soviet Union occupied the northern lands down to the 38$^{th}$ parallel and the United States occupied the south land below the 38$^{th}$ parallel. The main purpose for this was that both the United States and Soviet Union would be trustees and help both sides to work at becoming an independent country. The trustee positions changed when it was time to elect a way of government for the entire country. Kim Il Sung of North Korea decided not to vote but instead got the backing of Stalin and Mao Tse-tung to invade South Korea. Now all Kim Il Sung needed was a trigger to start the invasion. That trigger came when in 1950 Syngman Rhee, leader of South Korea, threatened the north with an invasion of his own. The trigger was pulled and war below the 38$^{th}$parallel began. The United Nations, with much support from the United States, declared war on North Korea, supporting the South. This war lasted three years and ended with an armistice which left North Korea at the 38$^{th}$ parallel, right where they started, and South Korea left at the 38$^{th}$ parallel, right where they started. There was a demilitarized zone set up which required a two kilometers' withdrawal on both sides from the 38$^{th}$. It was left like all countries after war. Thousands of soldiers, civilians and children dead. Those alive who started with a very meager lifestyle have now been leveled to complete ruin. There was no "win" in this war as far as territory. But the North Koreans were pushed back and the South regained its territory and its way of life. To this day, the South Koreans praise the United States for their support. South Korea has become one of our greatest allies in the area and has risen to a recognized industrial status in the world. The demilitarized zone is still a thorn in the side of international relations to this day. Since then the U.N. has made continuous efforts to meet with North Korea to no avail. Working for a compromise is still going on to this day.

# CHAPTER 16

*"Big Bear" - Max Sarazin – Heritage French - U.S. Marine*

## Life Before the War

Now here is a fellow that I wish you could all meet. He is a big teddy bear with a heart of gold. Not because he had a cushy life but despite hard times, he could always keep an open heart and mind. Then, the Korean War took shape and this teddy bear became a Marine and settled on Hill 407 along the Tae'dong River in doing his job.

Max's story starts with being born during the Great Depression. My first question was about his childhood. He said, "I did have a childhood, and it included a wind-up train that I played with for hours along with other childhood games of the day. My childhood lasted until the age of nine or ten. After that I worked the farm all summer, then after school and until I graduated high school." Max said, "I learned to work hard from the age of nine with my dad telling me 'Do it right the first time or you'll just have to do it again.'"

Life changes began when Max was eighteen. He said, "I was walking down the main road of my town, I stopped in front of Pettengill's store. I saw the headline of the Daily Record, written in big print, "North Korea Invades South Korea." It took only two weeks after graduation for me to join the Marines. So off to boot camp and the beginning of grow-up time."

## Life During the War

When I asked Max about boot camp, he replied, "One thing I will never forget in training was a surprise that greeted me when I crawled into my pup tent. Totally exhausted, I threw myself down on my bunk, when right next to my ear I heard a rattle, a hell of a rattle. There it was, right next to my left ear, looking right at me, a great big, ugly, mother of a rattle snake looking eye to eye with me and she was ready to strike." Nothing in the manual for this one.

"I was no John Wayne, my body froze. Every single muscle in my body tightened, like a spring on my pocket watch. That's all I remember, as I went into shock. Finally, when I came out of it, I just looked at my watch and it was 0200. I had been in that frozen position for three hours. The snake was gone and I was relaxed and quiet like nothing had just happened. Lesson learned, never sleep too soundly while in the service. You never know who your bed partner will be.

"The second memory that will never leave me, and I wasn't even in war with the enemy yet. It was the day I saw helicopters landing behind a building, in the northwest corner of the field. I went to investigate. As I approached, I saw these small Bell choppers. Man, they were a sight. Until I got a little closer and saw their cargo. Each machine had a litter on each side with the bloodiest mess I had ever seen. Soldiers returning from battle; all bloody and battered and in terrible pain. Limbs torn, torso opened, and heads battered. Reality set in. I heard a voice say **"What in Hell?"** I did not turn to see who had spoken. I knew it was me. It was my voice. I never had talked to myself before and I have never forgotten the first sight of war."

No time to process, transport is here and so off to Korea and Hill 407. He said, "First thing I saw on Hill 407 was an opening to a rat hole, a name we gave our living quarters while on the hill. The interior of this pit was lined with boards to avoid cave-in. The entrance was wide enough for the BC scope and for using Navy 50x20 binoculars. There was a drip heater in a drum to try and keep the cold out. The first night there, I slowly crawled into my cot, no damn coiled friends near my head tonight. Everything is fine, cozy, warm, comfortable and down for the night, until. . . **Damn! I have to pee!"** Had to crawl out of my warm sleeping bag to go out into the freezing twenty-below-cold night to relieve myself. I never got warm after that. But I did learn two things not in the manual. 'Do not sleep with snakes and do not pee in the night while in Korea.' It can take one minute for exposed flesh to freeze. Us guys are working in a cold, wet, sleepless, horrible environment. We have C-ration food from WWII and a rat hole for home. All I could do was pray for tomorrow."

He went on to explain his job, "The first thing we did was look at our surroundings, checked land marks (villages, roads, mountains) and identify them on the maps. Then coordinate these landmarks and begin a defense plan. We did not have tools of today like cell phones, computers electronics or eyes-in-the-sky drones. We used pencils, paper maps, AN/GRC-9 radios, and telephones with wire running the long distance to the CP (Command Post) in the valley.

We needed to be close enough to see the enemy in action. Our job was to give coordinates for fire support whenever needed. Our total focus became the enemy and his every move. At times, we were caught right in the middle of the action.

For seven months, in the main line of resistance, my job as part of the Air and Naval Liaison Company was to call in artillery and naval gunfire strikes from my position on good old 407 along the Tae'dong River. Due to my training as a kid - of 'do it right the first time and you won't have to repeat,' along with my advanced Marine training, I can tell you we very seldom missed our target."

Max and his crew were a bit luckier than those on hill 395. "Those guys were being slaughtered by the enemy. Thousands of the Chinese were overriding their position so that the lieutenant was yelling over the radio, 'Bomb us, bomb us. They are here, right here, we've been overrun, bomb us'"

Max said,' It really is the luck of the draw. That could have been us as easy as not."

Max did not stay on bad news too long. He said, "New note, once in a while we had a chance of making the long trek down to the CP to get a hot meal and possibly a hot shower. There was a real generator for a real refrigerator and real lights in the officer's mess and medical tents. Wow, get to relax with a real warm shower, but you can't count on a good time for long." The next thing Max said was, "We got strafed, enemy planes coming in. They were flying low and shooting at anything in the CP area. I could hear the gunfire before I saw the plane. It was a MIG-15 coming right at us. You would not believe the noise a 50-caliber machine gun makes when it is coming right up behind you, especially if it is at night with it being damp and little or no wind. I was one of the lucky ones, I was so damn lucky, there was a 6x6 (truck) close enough for me to dive under. Usually, once you hear the sound of that machine gun it's a little late to dive but I made it, and I could see their aim hitting the ground along side of me. Another day to wonder 'why not me.'

When the excitement was over, darkness was falling. It was time to head back to OP. I was feeling more myself after things settled down so I decided to take the short cut. A short cut that we were told **Do Not Take.** It was through a mine field, but my thinking and eyes were telling me right there in front of me was a well-defined path. A path that had no brush or debris whatsoever. So here I go. Half way up the path I'm doing fine and then I discover the reason for the sign. Lots of debris and no path ahead. As the path disappeared, I went on my hands and knees in the middle of a field of "bouncing betty's. The rest of the way, sweating with every move, very slowly feeling around, with my fingertips, for betty's prongs. It took me the longest short cut to finally reach the OP. A bouncing betty is a small bomb that if you step on the prongs, which is the only thing that is above ground, she will disable you into many, many little pieces. (The mine jumps from the ground to about waist-high before exploding.) "Third, lesson not in manual, don't mess with betty.

It finally came. We were told to hold our fire as a truce was about to happen. First the good news came. We got the word and rushed to get all the gear together and to destroy our happy rat hole of a home. We had 72 hours to get below the $38^{th}$ parallel. My gear was comprised of my shit list notebook, my training manual and all my dirty clothes. We all got ready to hurry up and wait, wait and wait.

Bad News, we were then told that the U.S. Navy couldn't get us out because the big doors wouldn't close on the LST down at Pyang'yang-do. Can you believe that? So, we continued to wait, and waited, and waited, and on the very last day for us to get out of enemy territory a South Korean rust bucket of an LST came and offered us a lift. We were rescued the day the North Koreans were taking over.

"We later caught a train which took as many hours as it did miles to get us to our destination. It was at that time, when I was walking down a dusty dirty Korean road to finally get a decent shower, I met a dirty-faced Marine. That dirty-faced Marine was Moe, my old classmate. Couldn't believe such luck. We hugged and then he took me to a tent where George, another classmate was. The three of us had the best reunion ever. One more thing the manual did not teach was, 'Don't be surprised at what you find on a dusty dirty road in Korea.', We all headed home together."

I asked Max what he learned from his experience.

He said laughing "Be careful who you sleep with, don't pee outside in the cold, don't mess with betty and never be surprised who you might meet in war."

## Life After the War

So Max is home and due to his early introduction to responsibility and work ethics he went on to graduate with highest honors at Northeastern University, then married and had two sons. Went on to become a pilot, to race a Falcon Class Sloop winning the 1971 Nationals and, last but not least, from a childhood love of wind-up trains, to his role as president of the Nauset Model Railroad Club.

May your God bless Max

Thanks for your service.

## Questions

1. What Reason for war

   He replied, "Power, wealth, and with every altercation religion is involved."

2. What was the role of Black Soldiers?
   "Black soldiers were treated about the same as whites in basic training. We were all called maggots or pukes by the Drill Instructor till we graduated. The southern maggots or pukes did not like the Yankee maggots or pukes. But it was in Korea that integration of troops began."
3. What was the role of women?
   His response on women and how they were treated was, "They were treated like the male marines, but in separate platoons. They were BAMS, standing for Beautiful American Marines, but we called them Broad Ass Marines, so they were renamed WM for Women Marines, but that just led to Walking Mattresses, but not in fact - only in name. Today they are Marines, no other name, just proud Marines."
4. What was the role of gays and lesbians?
   He said, "I never met any gays or lesbians. I did know there were some stationed in Pearl Harbor when we were at Camp Catlin."
5. What was the role of Native American?
   "Don't know. Never met any. I have a friend who says him and an Indian took a whole enemy position with just about four bullets left between them.
6. What was the role of the media?
   He said, "We were out of touch with any form of media. We received mail and provisions once a month when a replenished ship came back up the line carrying beans, bullets, and bandages."
7. What would you tell the youth of today?
   His response was, "good way to prepare them for life."
8. Would you do it again?
   "Absolutely."

# CHAPTER 17

*"Straight Talker" Paul Cobane – Heritage Irish - Marines*

This is the story of a kid who joined the Marines in 1947, at the age of seventeen, and returned home two years later paralyzed from his neck to his toes.

## Life Before the War

The first thing I did was asked for a quick synopsis of his childhood so I might understand his reason for joining the service at seventeen. He began with, "What I remember growing up was watching my dad going to work at the dairy plant, seven days a week. Mom did alterations at home along with caring for the house and us kids. I remember fun as a kid like hunting, fishing, ball games and skiing. I never drank, smoked or swore." He said, "It had nothing to do with religion or good or bad. It was the respect for hard work. I couldn't understand working hard for a dollar and then lighting it up."

The reason he decided to join the service at seventeen, with his mom's permission, was interesting, and I am sure it is something that happens to many young people. He said, "We walked two miles, no matter what the weather, to school and back. I felt energized whether rain, snow or sunshine. The two-mile hike made us strong. We developed muscle, strength, and endurance and I loved it. The love stopped when I entered the school. Things changed.

"I had no idea why. I respected all adults, never cheated and did all my assignments. I raised my hand a great deal, but I was never called on, but when it was kept down, the teacher would call on me, verbally belittle me in front of my whole class which seemed like an eternity with all my friends just watching. She did it over and over. She must have hated someone I reminded her of. She was really hateful to me. Maybe it was religion, nationality, or maybe just a reminder of a brother that made her so nasty. I never found out. I just realized that school was not for me, and that is how I ended up with a quick stop at Parris Island, S.C. for a basic training and then off to Guam at the age of seventeen."

## Life During the War

As a teenager he learned jungle warfare. He said, "We did 10- to 12-mile hikes every day. We learned assaults on hills with blank ammo, attacks on pill boxes with blank ammo, how to envelope an enemy position with blank ammo, attacks with use of 60mm mortars. We learned just about every warfare situation one can think of. We also swam with packs and rifles, learning to stay afloat doing the dog paddle. We were the highest trained that the Marines had, and we were proud of that." He said, "When training was over, I was a pretty grown-up 19-year-old."

I asked for an interesting fact about Guam that most people would not know, knowing that few American's even knew where Guam was.

Paul said, "Flying rats, that's what was over there, and a funny way of making coffee, and then there was the way we took a shower without cutting your feet."

He began explaining, "Flying coconut rats were native to the island along with unbelievable heat and all kinds of strange bugs. The rats lived in trees and they traveled. I mean they really traveled between trees on telephone and electric lines and therefore traveled into our Quonset huts. The beams in the huts were two inches or less in width and the rats would travel on them. When they tried to pass each other on the beams without enough room, one would fall down. So even with mosquito nets that we hung around us, we never were guaranteed no nightly visitors.

"Floors were the problem with the showers. They were made of jungle landing strips that slice like a razor. As careful as possible as you are, you could slip when you drop the soap or lose your balance. We needed to find some type of clog for our feet or no shower. The shower was a bucket of water that was warmed by the sun. It was a fast shower. We got to wear wooden clogs on our feet.

"Now the coffee, that was to be a luxury, was made in a big pot, a big copper vat that was filled with water. Then with a cheese cloth bag filled with coffee (no idea if it was used before or cleaned), was added to the big vat. It was then stirred with a wooden paddle that had pieces of wood that would float onto the coffee. Now every guy there would use their canteen to dip in and fill it with coffee. Canteens with no cleaning and a hundred mouths drinking out of them. It was not the Starbucks of the day. I opted for the organic tin tasting orange juice that we could buy at the PX. A case of 24 tin cans (left over from WWII) cost us 25 cents."

So now he does not swear, smoke, drink or even have coffee. If he can make it through the war, he should live a long life.

"The year was 1950 and the month was February, and we were heading home. Believe me, we were happy to have our feet on solid ground. We were taking great showers, eating good food, and de-stressing after Guam. Just as we were beginning to enjoy life, we hear the word war. The war was called the Korean War and we were heading into it. August 3,1950, and we're landing in Buson three weeks after the war started. I saw those poor soldiers that had to hold North Koreans back until reinforcement arrived. With no equipment and no experience those young lives saved the day. If they hadn't South Korea would have been lost.

"When I first landed in Buson I was part of a Fire Brigade due to the fact there were not enough Marines to make up a division. The first thing I learned was there are no rules in war. Found it out the hard way. A young kid age eight or nine came walking towards us. Arms in the air, fear on his face, and a grenade between his knees. We didn't see it till it was too late. That little kid opened his legs. He blew himself up and caused damage. Not only physical but emotional. Not every day you expect to see a kid blown apart." At that age, he was no more. I feel bad that kids need to get involved in war and grenades do not differentiate by age. But as Paul said, "It just shows that the politicians sitting in their air conditioned offices making rules like 'don't hurt civilians,' really are just making a big mess out of it." He continued by saying, "Now, I'm told that in this year of 2017, even if you are being shot at you need permission to shoot back, by some general in his office. There are no rules in war but to stay alive. That's my belief."

I asked him what happened next. He replied, "After I saw what that young kid did, I realized in order to survive this war I was going to shoot at anything that moves and sometime even things that I shouldn't have. That is what war is."

We took a breath. I asked about any battles he was in. He replied, "Me and Lloyd Green, a Hopi Indian and who was an unbelievable fighter, are side by side going up Hill 101 on the Langton River. We are shooting anything that moves and everything that moves keeps moving back.

We get to the top and the gooks are running up the next hill like crazy. We keep shooting like it was a turkey shoot. I end up with a clip (eight bullets) and Lloyd ended with one bullet in the chamber of his rifle. We get up and turn. We are all alone. Not another Marine there. Not a single sound. We look at each other in total confusion. Without a word we start down the hill and hear 'Oh you two didn't hear. The attack was called off. The North Koreans started to break through the lines just to the east and they needed our support there.' So much for good communication. I don't believe Lloyd or I would have it any other away."

Soon after, they were pulled off the front lines. Paul said, "We were heading for Inchon. I was going to be the flag raiser of Inchon like the guys did in Iwo Jima. I had my little American flag tucked onto my backpack. It was 6:30 a.m. and we were the first wave of the Inchon Landing at Wolmi-Do. It wasn't an easy trip since a typhoon decided to keep us company. A hundred of us guys were sleeping in the mess hall, and I was the lucky one because I got to hang onto the pole that held the dinner trays. The waves were so high that the front of the ship was totally under at times.

"Within ten minutes of landing, my little American flag was all torn and attached to some barbwire and someone was yelling grenade. I dropped. I can hear something rolling. In my head I am saying please, please be rolling the other way. It blew. My body jumped up and down. I couldn't breathe. I kept trying to get my breath. Once I collected myself, I found out that it was an old Japanese grenade, and it was called a concussion grenade. Its purpose was to blow up your brains along with coloring everything around it green. So, I am lucky I still have my brains but I am covered with green. So now I end up green, the ground around me green, and my little famous flag is all green. It was torn, tattered and green. So much for my fame at Inchon."

Paul settled for a second and then began. "Our company of Marines, H35, left Wolmi-Do during the night of September 15 and went across the causeway in the dark - into the city of Inchon and dug in on the northeastern edge of Inchon for the balance of the night. Then on to Seoul in the following days.

Next obstacle was the Han River which was west of Seoul where we dug in for the day waiting for Amtracs (LTV (3)C, a tracked landing vehicle) to get us across the river. I don't remember the day of the crossing, but we got to Hill 296 on the outskirts of Seoul on September 21$^{st}$ or 22$^{nd}$. I remember being in the first Amtrac to the river and remembering grinding up a gook in a rice paddy just across the river."

It is now September 23 and the weather was awful, and the battle was going strong. Paul then says, "I'm done. We are at the battle of Seoul and a mortar goes off right behind me. I hear a voice yell 'Cobane's hit Cobane's hit.' I'm lying there and not feeling a thing. Not a thing. So, I'm thinking lucky again. That was till I tried to move. When I tried to move I couldn't. I was nineteen years old on the battlefield, in a foreign country and totally paralyzed. If it were not for the corpsman, who put his finger, knuckle deep, into my neck, I would be dead. If this did not happen to me, I would have been on my way to the battle of Chosin. Later, hearing what happened there, guess I was a bit better off than some guys who became prisoners or lay frozen along the side of the reservoir. I was airlifted to Tokyo Army Hospital the same day and it was there that, even in the paralyzed condition I was in, I saw the most beautiful nurse.

"As I was being lifted out of a 'Bus,' I was thinking, I am coming back here and find her. I can still see her. Remember I am only nineteen, so what can I say." The other guys were screaming in pain because of wounds that they could feel. The bus trip was not a luxury Greyhound but an old bus with bad brakes, bad shocks and bad springs. I was lucky. I couldn't feel a thing."

## Life After the War

When he reached Tokyo, "I was treated like royalty by the aids at the hospital. The aids were Japanese girls. They were petite seventeen or eighteen years old and so very polite. Dressed in light blue tops (smocks). They had peaked white or blue caps. They would keep saying 'you Marine, you Marine' and then proceeded to spend hours around me caring and washing me almost constantly. It was then that I found out that I could move a toe. I could move one toe. There was hope."

I am so surprised that after so much happening that he still has a great sense of humor. He continues with, "It was at Army Trippler Hospital in Honolulu when I finally got my hair washed." After months of wearing a little jungle on his head which consisted of dirt, twigs, and unknown things, he gets his hair washed. He said, "I was in a bed where the middle of the bed raised up. My head was considerably lower than the rest of my body. A rubber sheet was put under my head and shoulders and funneled into a bucket on the floor. It was crucial not to move my head so the doc held my head in a steady position, and the army medic along with aids began to tell me what they found in my hair. Comments like 'what is this, eek, guess what.' They made it an adventure for me. The only part of me that could feel, along with my big toe, was my head and let me tell you that it was the most calming peaceful feeling when they were through." The jungle was gone and he said, "I felt so clean and so human again."

"Last stop before I am discharged was St. Albans naval hospital where I continued with physical therapy and occupational therapy. It was so good to be on familiar ground that I called home."

After all the re-union hugs and settling down, I asked what next?

He said, "It was then that my mother took a pair of tweezers and began taking shrapnel, stones, and dirt out of my back. It was nearly two years that I had spent recovering. I was discharged from the hospital the same day as my discharge from the Marines. I was still very disabled with many more recovery needed to be addressed."

I asked about mobility, hand functioning. He replied, "I could and can walk, but as then and today I don't walk as I could before being wounded. I wobble all over when walking. I think it unlikely that I will be in any parades soon.

"I could not utilize my hands very well due to lack of feelings. I tried for work and one job was putting shingles on a house. But several days later I was fired. I could not pick up the nails fast enough.... for the boss. Next was a senior counselor and riflery program teaching the handling of guns for 13- to 17-year-old kids. Then I headed for college and the counseling job ended.

"I found happiness with my second wife, who I had known briefly in college. We had both gone our separate ways, had both been married, both were single now. When I found her in 2003, she was single again? I had been searching for months for her. Very difficult since she had a different name. After all I had gone through, I knew I was due for a win, and I was. I found her, married her and now am living the good life."

## Questions:

1. Why do we have wars?
   "Politicians!"
2. Was there any media coverage of the war?
   "Very little . . . Nothing like today."
3. What do you think about women being in the front lines?
   "Bad idea."
4. Did you work with any Black individuals?
   "I don't think I ever saw a black Marine in the four years I was in the Marines, and I never had any around in any job I ever worked at."

5. Did you work with any Native American Indians?
   "Loyd Green, Hopi Indian. Discussed him in my story."
6. How were gays treated?
   "It was never said or shown that there was public knowledge."
7. How was PTSD treated?
   "Shell shock!!! As in WWII. Sorry, that was it."
8. What would you tell young people today about joining?
   "Do it, you cannot buy the experience."
9. Would you do it again?
   "Yes."

# CHAPTER 18

*"The-Walking Library" Larry Cole - Heritage English - Army*

## Life Before the War

He is a walking library. He is the Korean vet that has been introducing me to other veterans for interviews, books to read, movies to see, along with his own opinions on presidents, politics and his life experience as a soldier in the Korean War. Not only is his mind sharp, but his body is still running marathons. I should mention he is eighty-three.

This was the second time I met Larry, and I could tell by his manner and the tone of his voice that he was upset. So, as I poured coffee, I let him speak. He said "The New York Times just published a review article on a museum exhibition about WWI, and the reviewer proceeded to elaborate on how WWI which was the precursor of WWII, Vietnam, The Gulf War, etc., in terms of technologies deployed and tactics used. But he did not cite the salient feature of WWI, which was trench warfare, and that was what the last two years of Korea was like. That was never a feature of WWII, Vietnam, The Gulf War, Iraq, or Afghanistan. The reviewer never mentioned The Korean War. Again, the Korean War, the 'Forgotten War' has been left out."

He was angry because he had just told me the day before, "You are putting too much emphasis on Korea being a forgotten war. I think that might have changed a bit" and now, one day later, he said "Go for it, write as much as you want about forgotten."

Guess people still need reminding of young kids that lost their youth in rat infested, muddy trenches while risking their lives for democracy.

Larry and his fellow Korean veterans have a right to be angry. Some joined, and some were drafted in the 1950s. Many were seventeen or eighteen years old and had just graduated from high school and were wet behind their ears. Some of them hadn't had their first shave, first drink, first date or even their first cigarette, let alone hear of Korea or even know where Korea was. Many did not even understand why they were there. But they were there. To this day they have continued to pay a hero's price for their wartime in Korea. They are still living with vivid memories of war-torn countryside, fellow soldiers dying, civilians starving.

They then came home to statements like "Hey where you been?" "What you been up to?" So, you might understand why Larry and fellow veterans are a little upset.

Just another quick addition from Larry's political view on what makes veterans upset. "A lot of guys grew up wanting to believe John Wayne was more than a movie hero, but when it came time to sign-up, he took a back seat when other actors were signing to fight." He also said, "The younger Bush, to avoid being drafted and becoming a grunt, jumped ahead of the line and went into the Texas Air National Air Guard. After young Bush received lots of very expensive pilot training, he declined the opportunity to fly in Vietnam, so he could campaign for a candidate for the US Senate. Then years later he plops down on an aircraft carrier in his jump suit and proclaims 'Mission Accomplished' in the Iraq War. It was hard to reconcile this with his father's exemplary behavior in WWII."

As I was sipping my coffee, I decided to move to a more relaxed area of questioning. I asked about his youth. Larry answered, "My life was good back when I was young, and I was a pretty good kid at the time." As he continued to talk, I figured out why he was such a good kid. He said, "I worked in my father's country general store in Vermont, which he managed with only a partial high school education, my mother was the town clerk, and my aunt was the teacher of the one-room schoolhouse." No wonder Larry was such a good kid, he had nowhere to go to be a bad kid. He said, "I did all the kids' things like skiing, fishing, swimming, but after the WWII started, we began playing soldiers in the fields and woods, and would go in one kid's family's barn with a ladder straight up to the loft (conning tower) and played submarine. Little did I know that the time would come when I would be a soldier in a real war, with real bullets and real enemies.

"I was in my senior year of high school when the Korean War broke out. After flubbing my freshman year, and the draft being imminent, I decided to get it over with and join the Army. Before he knew it, I was enlisted, trained, and shipped over to the Pusan Peninsula in Korea. In March of 1953, it was nothing like playing soldier in that old barn in New England, USA."

## Life During the War

He said, "First thing I remember was seeing the terribly crowded and primitive living conditions in Pusan, which was teeming with refugees from farther north, looking at the lower than poverty level that these people lived in, I remember the pity I felt for them. No other word but retched can describe it. They appeared in what I would describe as rags, without the means to get clean and they were definitely being undernourished."

Larry began talking about the terrain he was in. "The terrain just got hillier as we traveled up north on a train that moved slow as molasses and had wood slats for seats. I saw people working rice paddies that stunk like hell. Others, especially children, followed the train trying to sell fruit to the soldiers. So many refugees. Second thing I remember was being told 'do not eat the fruit'. The why of it was that the people use human feces to fertilize their crops."

Talk about poor.

"The train took us to a little town northeast of Seoul, it was called Uijonbu, were the 45$^{th}$ Infantry Division replacement depot was located. At that time, the unit that I had been assigned to was attached to the 45$^{th}$ Division. After a couple of days of processing, those of us going to the 5$^{th}$ Regimental Combat Team headed east to report into companies that had just come off the front in the Punch Bowl. The late spring weather was cold and windy. It was not unlike that of southern New Hampshire that time of year, so it was not a shock to me, but it was a struggle for some of the southern fellows, since they were not accustomed to it.

Within a day or two, the whole Regimental Combat Team was westward bound to become attached to the 3rd ID, and this move set a pattern of making fourteen east-west moves in sixteen weeks, wherever the regiment was needed to plug a hole in the line or act in blocking or reserve capacity for other divisions. Blocking is part of defense in depth, and reserves are available as reinforcement to be moved when needed."

Since, the North Korean and/or Chinese trenches were not that far from their position, Larry said, "We would go out and set ambushes for their patrols or sneak up and try to identify their positions of trench lines or where their guns were situated. We would move out in the dark and penetrate the enemy lines to gather intel on what their next move will be. Sometime patrols would take a prisoner back for interrogation to see what could be learned about the enemy's intentions.

One night, it was pitch black and the wind was silent, we could almost hear the bullets coming our way. The sergeant behind me, a three-time Purple Heart veteran of WWII named Hart, got shot in the back. Now as I remember, with help from two soldiers, they got him back to safety. We had called ahead where a medic would be waiting for him." He said, "I'm beginning to think we survive on luck, just luck. That bullet was close enough that it could have been mine."

I asked Larry why the battle of Pork Chop Hill was so important that so many young lives were given to gain that hill. He said, "The battle of Pork Chop began in April of '53, and at that time, the negotiations at Panmunjom, for peace, were in a critical phase. The US Command decided it couldn't afford to allow the Chinese to come to the talks with a second recent victory, after they had decided to stop contesting the adjacent hill, Old Baldy.

The Communists were testing the UN to see how many lives it would spend to hold onto a position, such as Pork Chop Hill. Their assaults were preceded by huge artillery and mortar shelling of small patches of ground, but in the end Pork Chop was held. The price in lives was at a considerable cost to the 7th ID infantrymen."

I had talked to Larry about the Battle at the Chosin Reservoir, because we had read that four companies of 250 men each went up the hill and only twelve men returned. It was a battle we did not win. Young boys eighteen, nineteen, or twenty who had never been further than their home town, who had been raised to do good, do no harm, do not kill, have seen minefields with dozens of men scattered across the field, all of which now are dead or badly wounded.

Please don't say real men don't cry. Real men, when they see their friends shot, bleeding, dying, and crying for home, they cry. They cry because they can do nothing else but hold their friends until the dying soldier closes his eyes. Those who were captured walked miles in frigid weather with no shoes, gloves, food, only to end up as POWs in the worst Chinese prisons ever.

Do you think they cry?

Just asking.

Larry said, "McArthur disobeyed the president's orders to stay away from the Chinese border. The Chinese had warned President Truman if we moved closer to their border that they would attack. McArthur continued to move forward and the Chinese did attack. McArthur had ignored his orders and that was his downfall. He was fired.

Larry mentioned, "that in the same book, Chosen, it talked about our soldiers, as bad as they had it, feeling worse for the enemy prisoners. They came over the mountains without shoes, jackets, food or rifles. Their feet were covered with blocks of ice. One soldier said some of these enemy were just every day farmers or daily workers with families like us."

"I really believe names like dago, harp, nigger, beano, kraut, chink or wetback become useful when we take the human out of the enemy, then the enemy becomes not human. Easier to kill.

What do you think?

Just asking.

## Life After the War

We ended the interview by my asking Larry how he stays so positive and young at heart and he replied, "The way I keep my body, mind, and soul intact is by running the occasional marathon along with 45-50 races per year for my body, working as scribe for my veterans' organization (KWVA) and along with reading for my mind, and for my soul I listen to jazz and classical music along with a fine glass of wine, good food, once in a while in the company of a young lady on my arm and, last but not least, plenty of ice cream."

## Questions

1. What is the reason for war?
   He said, "Human greed, the quest for control, dominance and power, often in the form of ego trips on the part of rulers. Mad men in power, as in North Korea. Also, war is resorted to as a diversion from failure to deliver on the domestic front." He then added "When wars are, in retrospect, regarded as having been blunders, ignorance is often the root, as is frequently the case in human problems."
2. How women in the service were treated:
   "Only women there were nurses and they were all in hospitals, so unless you need medical care, you didn't see them."
3. How did he think black soldiers were treated.
   "Truman ordered the armed services to integrate in 1947-8. It didn't take effect all at once, so early in the war there were some all black combat arms units committed to the fight which didn't perform very well. They were split up and assigned in small groups to many other units, which solved the performance problem. By the time I entered the Army there were black officers and NCO's in command positions, and their orders were obeyed like any others. Some support units, such as transportation companies, were still largely black and that took a little longer to unwind. The only thing I heard that was still segregated was the prostitutes in Japan who serviced the black vets were different than the ones who serviced the whites."

4. As far as gays and lesbians?
   Larry said, "Back then the males were 'fags' or 'queers' and they were punished when found out. They were objects of derision and eventually given a dishonorable discharge. The discharge would be the punishment that followed from a court martial. They would probably lose all veteran's benefits as well."
5. Any media coverage?
   "The media was non-existent, except for The Stars and Stripes."
6. How was PTSD handled?
   "The truth is some veterans come back with suicidal thoughts, drug addicted, or end up homeless because of PTSD."
7. What would you tell youth today?
   He stated that he would tell today's youth, "Don't go just because you can't find or get a better job, unless it is to pay for education afterward. There are other ways to grow up. Better have a clear career goal in mind and get trained/schooling accordingly. Be in good physical condition upon entry, and don't shy away from getting help on active duty in dealing with problems brought on by job, stress or trauma. As a matter of fact, I am presently helping my great-grandson to make up his mind about what he wants to do after high school graduation this year, if he wants college or military."
8. As for doing it again Larry replied
   "At my age, I don't have to consider it, but if you mean was it worth it, or do I consider either the war itself, or my going in, a mistake, then, in my view the war was justified, and nothing is more persuasive than what South Korea has become, and what it has escaped by not being ruled by North Korea. As for me personally I'm glad to have had the military experience in general, and in particular to have participated in South Korea's defense, drawing the line on overt aggression, and signaling Moscow, and Beijing that Communism was not going to be the uncontested wave of the future."

# CHAPTER 19

*"Gentleman Jones" Stanley Jones- Heritage English - Army*

When I first met Stanley, he reminded me of a Cary Grant kind of guy. He kind of walks with a dignified pace, with a purpose. He has a gentle tone to his voice and a calmness in his manner. Unlike Cary Grant, the movie star, Stanley did not act 'life' he lived it for real. He became New England's backstroke swimming champ in 1947. He also did other competitive sports such as football and track. To this day, at 84 he still continues to swim.

## Life Before the War

Stanley grew up during the depression era where little was extra and nothing was free. Getting a new pair of shoes was not a given but a gift. He said, "I was lucky because my dad had a job as purchasing agent. He would dress in a white shirt, fitted suit, tie and a nice hat and dress shoes, and go off to work. My mother was a stay-at-home mom. Back then stay-at-home mothers used a wringer washer, clothes line and an icebox that kept perishables fresh up to 24 hours at a time. There were no frozen foods, and very few canned foods, so she would go to market every day. I still remember her taking a break. She would lean against the railing on the porch. She wore her printed house dress with a bib apron over it. She would light her cig from a fifteen-cent pack of Phillip Morris, with a wooden match, and then take a deep breath. I can still remember it so clear.

"Like all families during the war we received government gas coupons, two and a half gallons a week, canned goods were blue coupons, and the one for meat was red. We were doing much better than most."

That deep inhale and exhale of a cigarette is what I call a stay-at-home mom's work break, and the only stress reduction plan for women in the 40's.

When asked about his youth he said, "As religion goes, we were moderately active but the rule my parents gave me to live by was 'Do unto others as you want done unto you.' I was never encouraged to fight, as a matter of fact I was never taught.

"I was pretty secure and I had a pretty average life. I do remember my dad taking me up town one day when I was only five and I got to shake hands with a real Native American Indian who had fought in the war of 1880.This was a big deal to a five-year-old, since playing cowboys and Indians with friends was the game of the times. It's still a big deal to me today.

"We did well enough, during the depression, that my parents could even afford a new pair of shoes for me to start school. That was the highlight of my day." Back then you got a pair of shoes and they lasted until the sole wore out, and then they were resoled or cardboard was the new insole.

That day in class Stanley began to understand what depression was for kids who lived at the other end of town. It was a little different. He learned about the 'have's' and 'have nots.'

"At bathroom break I was surrounded by the bullies in my class and one by one they began to pee all over my new shoes." I asked what his parents or his teacher did. He simply replied, "Never thought of telling anyone."

You see back then kids took a lot of grief and very rarely complained to adults. There was an attitude back then that 'If it doesn't kill you it makes you stronger." No helicopter parents back then.

## Life During the War

This quiet Cary Grant guy, who was taught to do unto other as you want done unto you, was now in the Army and stationed in Korea freezing his butt off. His job was that of a ballistic meteorologist. A ballistic meteorologist may sound like a sit-down safe job, but actually it is a very dangerously needed entity for zeroing in on enemy targets and saving many of the lives of our troops. That was Stanley's job and the job of the twelve men under him. I asked if he could put it into layman language. He said, "We needed to have the physical endurance to perform activities without rest. We would monitor weather such as conditions and patterns so artillery could fire and promote missile accuracy.

"We were without computers, I-phones, or calculators. We used an old lead pencil and paper and needed to add numbers in our head. We needed to think and remain calm under stress. Times when we were stationed on one of the highest mountains in Korea, living in a tent, in frigid weather, and eating C-rations. We needed to be on constant alert for enemy planes and ground forces. The terrain was constantly guarded by patrols, along with barbed wire and trip flairs. Our tent had an oil stove along with an oil drum. If we turned the heat up, we would burn the tent down, and if we turned the heat down, we would freeze the coupling that was attached."

During one interview Stanley had spread out pictures that he had taken during his stint in Korea. Before we could even start talking, I glanced at a picture on the table. It was of a naked man and so my response: "So who's posing for Playgirl?" With a modest grin Stanley answered, "Well, it's my backside. I was on hill 108, which got to be 20+ below, and in order to wash you must move quickly. You fill your helmet with water and heat it on a little oil stove. With the same bar of soap, you use to do your clothes, your hair, and even wash your coffee cup, you begin to wash yourself as fast as you can, at times leaving out shaving, teeth brushing or nail clipping, and anything else that needed cleaning. It was just too damn cold. Your water not only gets cold, it freezes, so doesn't your butt."

Another story Stanley told me was, "It was Thanksgiving and (I) felt my crew needed a break, myself included, so we 'requisitioned' *a* truck and headed out to see a movie on a nearby air base. Keep in mind that it was in the 50's and the road to Kimpo was dirt. There were no street lights. It was totally black. So black you couldn't even see your hand in front of your face. The truck lights were your only guide.

"Now I had to take a wiz and since no toilets, I decide to pull the truck over and tell the guy 'I'll just jump out do my business and be right back.' I jump out, land on solid ground, so far so good. I cannot see a foot in front of me so I go slow. First step ok, second step just the same. It was the third step that took me flying into the air. I tumbled, scraped, rolled and flew down a 30-foot embankment. Oh shit, I ended up with grit fragments embedded in my hands, my knee was a roll back, along with part of my leg, and I ended up with blood poisoning."

Now was that some price for a wiz? Just asking

"But I can't complain due to the fact if I had landed a few inches either way I might have been just cut in half by the plane that had been shot down by the enemy."

Now that would really have been a hell of a price just for a wiz.

All of a sudden, Stanley has a very serious expression on his face. He starts with, "We got back to the base and bad news waited. My long-time buddy Benny is sitting with a bottle in one hand and a letter in the other. I have never seen my friend so demoralized. He looked at me with the emptiest eyes I had ever seen, and he handed me the letter. It seems his wife was pregnant and my friend Benny had been fighting this shitty war for over twelve months There is no fairness in this world, there just isn't."

There are many battles young soldiers fight before they reach the enemy. The tension is great, at times they are hanging on by a thread. A letter like that can end up in a wounded soldier's hand, or one fighting in a trench, or one devastated over a best buddy just dying. Where is the brain of a person who would send a 'Dear John' to someone hanging on by a thread?

## Life After the War

Stanley returned home with the Good Conduct Medal, the AM Defense Award, the US Korean Service Award, and the Korean Service V.N.

He went home, married his sweetheart, returned to his job in sales, and is currently a part of the Cape and Islands Chapter 1. When his tour of duty was over the service discharged Stanley. But Stanley never did truly discharge the service. He is the presently the Commander of the Cape and Islands of the Korean War Veterans Association. He just gave a presentation, in uniform, at the Korean War Monument in Hyannis, Mass. Just yesterday 7-27-17. Due to the decline of Korean veterans, the Cape and Islands Chapter 1 transferred the monument upkeep to the Town of Barnstable.

God Bless You Stanley Jones S/Sgt. Ballistic Meteorologist

## Questions

1. Reason for War?
   "Political"
2. Were there women in your war?
   "There are physical differences. A Colonel from West Point reported on women's physical differences and said basically it is hand strength. So, nothing against women but how can a 120-lb. woman carry me out if I'm wounded?"
3. What did you think of media coverage?
   "There was no media."
4. What about black soldiers?
   "Everyone was treated equal and they all did their jobs."
5. What would you tell young kids today?
   "Boys join right after high school and before college. They will mature much faster. As far as girls, I cannot imagine a girl wanting to join.'
6. What did you know about gays/lesbians in the service?

"I never knew if anyone was gay. There were no lesbians. Had great friends that were gay. We just all knew the limits."

7. How was PTSD handled?

   no answer

8. Would you do it again?

   "Yes.

# CHAPTER 20

*"Huffy" Frank Hufnagel - Heritage Irish-German - Army*

## Life Before the War

Frank, nickname Huffy, during school years, was a little on the wild side. Not on the bad side, just enough to enjoy his adolescence.

Family history first, Frank said, "I loved my dad. To me he was very strong. He was the head of the house and us kids knew a certain look or a tap on the head meant shape up.

"Dinner was on the table the same time every night and we would eat what was on our plate and never complain. Dad would then listen to the radio news. He was a frugal man and taught his kids to be the same. Mom was Irish Catholic and made sure we all went to Mass on Sunday."

I asked for a childhood memory and Frank replied, "I got a sled. It was the first gift and the one I remember most. Me and my buddies would get ready for the first snow, grab our leggings, rubber boots, stocking hat and Flexible Flyer sleds. We would then head for the road. Because it was set that we could have half the road but cars could still come up the hill. It was great for us because we would coast down and then grab the bumper of a car heading up. Those were the best years.

"You, your sled, your best friends, and childhood. It was heaven and we loved it."

Then 1952 appeared and graduation was at hand. Frank said high school was also a bit of heaven. There were girls, sports, drums and cars.

"I was never very interested in furthering my education. I was thinking fireman, or policeman, or street car conductor like my dad. It was 1952 when my heavens toppled and my feet landed firmly on the ground. The Korean War had begun. A place that us kids knew little about, and it was about to happen to us.

You see my brother Billy had been drafted and a good friend of mine had just come home from the war.

He came home with burns. Burns all over his face, and arms. The burns were caused by a flame thrower. This piece of equipment would be strapped on the soldier's back and when he would press a handle flames would stream out and burn anything or anyone in its way. My friend's job was that of a flame-thrower and something went wrong.

## Life During the War

"Well, there go my plans," said Frank. "Forget the fireman or police or street car conductor. I was going to become a soldier at eighteen years old. From heaven to hell in one short trip. It was a quick decision, a quick physical, and a quick trip to Basic Training Army camp. Next is to embark on my first sea journey."

So, how did you enjoy the ocean. He said, "We bounced up and down, two and fro, up and down, and back and forth for the whole 32 days. The only other entertainment we had during that time, besides all us guys turned green and watching each other take turns puking everywhere, we boxed for a carton of cigarettes. I went to watch a bout or two. One of the guys that went into the ring was a buddy of mine. What I saw when he got out of the ring made a super impression on me. I decided to smoke my cigarettes real slow and save my physically fit body for the enemy.

From Seattle, Washington to Yakama, Japan, then down to Sasebo, Japan, and then finally landing in Inchon, Korea. It was there that I thought I would lose my first battle even before seeing the enemy. I can't swim you see, so when they lowered the LSD craft and into the ocean I go. I really felt one more inch and I would be buried at sea because the ocean was right at the tip of my nose. I finally won that battle. Now with my feet on land, with my rifle and gear, I am ready to fight."

It was interesting to watch Frank grin and tell the next memory.

"With two hours of rice paddies, mountains all around, and roads made of dirt, travelling in a deuce-and-a-half. We reach our destination and we line up for introduction to our new sergeant.

The sergeant asked if we had any questions. I raised my hand and asked when could we take a shower since we were full of dirt and dust from the trip up. The look he gave me told me never to ask him a question, again. He then walked up to me and took my helmet and without a word marched me down to the water, the whole squad following me. I know at that moment he is thinking what a stupid, silly private. He proceeded to fill my helmet, and with a voice you cannot ignore he said 'This is your shower kid, You're not in Hyde Park anymore.' Right then and there I learned, that day, never ask questions ever. It then took six months before I got to the Xcorps to get my very first shower. I forgot how nice warm water that just keeps running felt. I did not want to ever come out.

This was not my worst happening on my first 24 hours. As a matter of fact, it was nothing compared to my first night. I was first assigned to the 40th infantry division. As a combat infantry soldier, up on the DMZ area I would go several patrols and then return and have guard duty sometime at night.

First night myself and a Korean soldier pulled first night patrol around the mess tent. Half way through our duty we hear a shot. It was not an enemy soldier. Myself and the Korean soldier, found a young soldier dead. He was not the enemy. He had played Russian Roulette with his fully loaded gun. He had just received a Dear John. He was nineteen. Before this young man's brain had fully developed, he just blew it up. It was the emotional killer that we were not trained to fight."

Frank said, "We are trained for physical war but never ready for this type of emotional combat. I was raised a Catholic which was do no harm, and then I was trained to kill and hate the enemy because they will kill you.

We were right on the DMZ at a place called Churion, with the 'fight or flight' syndrome with us every moment of the day and night. In order to try and get some release, we began talking about Thanksgiving in our tent. We decided to draw straws to see who would go on this mission to steal canned turkeys. Of course, I drew the short straw.

"So, it is night and dark and even though the distance from us and the turkeys was only about a hundred yards, it was very scary and it was guarded. So, I maneuvered my way through the hundred yards that to me seemed to be a hundred miles. It was so dark that I couldn't see my hand in front of my face. I watched the guard go around the corner and I slipped under the tent, grabbed the canned turkeys, and got my butt out in seconds flat. Again, a hundred miles back to our location. Like a bunch of kids, we settled into our tent and let out a few nervous laughs. When we opened the can much to my chagrin, I did not have a turkey. I had two cans of lard. That is when we ended up laughing so hard our stomachs hurt. No turkey but a great release and a promise to check a little more carefully before our next heist.

"My second mission was with the 2nd Infantry Division which was an operations and intelligence Battalion level (S2+S3) We were across the DMZ line and we could see the enemy. We were posted on a platform, high up on stilts. We would climb a ladder a very high ladder with our rifle ready and when on top we would proceed to view the landscape for enemy action. Our purpose was to draw out rear area defense plans along with interpret aerial photographs. Then we would contact Headquarters and report our findings. I still feel the cold in my bones from spending two winters in "Frozen Chosin" Korea.

## Life After the War

"I returned home from war and thanked God. I was so lucky. I married my beautiful green-eyed beauty, Elizabeth. We had three sons and one daughter. I went to college under the G.I Bill. I became an Industrial Arts Teacher for thirty years. Twenty of them on Cape Cod, Massachusetts."

## Questions

1. Why do you think we had your war?
   "Communism is a belief that all is for the common good. Joseph Stalin, our ally, in World War II was a dictator. A dictator that

killed thousands of his own people or he sent them to Siberian prison camps if they did not accept his doctrine. He believed in world domination by Russia through communism.

"The United States called that the domino theory and that was the reason we needed to stop them in Korea. North Korea was under the influence of Russia and the south was protected by the United Nations. We did not want to see the domino theory effect to continue swallowing up one country after another."

2. What do you think of women in the service?
   "We were all treated the same."
3. How about African Americans in the service?
   "Not like in WWII. Integration had begun."
4. What about Native Americans in the service?
   "We were all treated the same?"
5. What about the treatment of gay people in the service?
   "I never knew if I was sleeping in a tent with a gay guy or not. I slept just fine."
6. What would you tell youth today?
   "To my young friends. If you love your country and it needs your help because someone is trying to take away your liberties then you should help. Help by joining the military. I do not regret one day of my Army service. Young men and women, if you want to learn a lot about our beautiful country, enlist."
7. Was there any media coverage of the war?
   "Yes, our country was very patriotic at that time."
8. Would you do it again?
   "Without a doubt. Many countries with a communism or radical Muslim belief would love to destroy our country. We have a choice either surrender or fight for liberty".
9. How was PTSD handled?
   "I just talked to my buddies if I had a problem. Life goes on."

**Letter Home- When the enemy helped**

My Dearest Wife & Family,

Just a line to let you know I have been wounded and am in the hospital in Japan. I was shot through the right thigh with a single sniper bullet. I am thankful to be alive.

We had to break up a road block near Hakchon where 300 Chinese were supposed to have been dug in; they had a regiment of the 3rd division cut off and we had to make contact with them without delay. Everything was thrown at them before the infantry try and tanks went in – planes, artillery, and mortars in big doses. Then the 3rd Bn. Went in with "L" Co. on tanks. I was on a tank about 8 minutes -- then I was hit. I screamed at them to stop the tank so I could get off and crawl into a ditch. Taylor of my squad also got wounded while helping to carry me out. After Taylor got hit there was not enough men to carry me, so they dropped me and said they would send help or come back with more help. I lay there for a short while and then dragged myself about ten yards to a little better cover, and I lay there till well after dark.

I saw some guys walking around against the dim light of the sky. I yelled for help again, and they started toward me; they had long fixed bayonets, and by their . . . [Line or more of text is missing from the original letter.]

a Chinese medic came and put a fresh bandage on my leg and put me in a litter. I was carried into the one house that was left standing where they made a warm fire and covered me up as best they could. My wet clothes made it very difficult for me to get warm but I am sure that what they did for me saved my life.

American artillery and mortar shells were landing in the general area all night long. They (the Chinese) left about 2:00 o'clock.

I waited until about one o'clock in the afternoon and a GI patrol came in to give the village the once-over. I opened the door and yelled for help. This time they heard me and found me. I thanked God! In less than five minutes I had a drink of water, a morphine shot, a cigarette, and a fresh bandage on my leg, and a litter jeep on the way to pick me up. . ..

Well, I am going to close for now, my darling, and will try to write again tomorrow. I think it would be proper and fitting if you would let as many of the family and friends as possible read this letter.

I love you and have an idea that I will be seeing you soon.

Love to all,
Paul

P.S. What's left of the squad would still like to have your cookies!

## Weapons

Since the war was only a short time after the end of WWII many of the weapons used were the same, with a few new or improved battle machines. The new weapons that entered the world arena were: The Centurion, the Super Bazooka, Jet Dogfights, and Helicopters for large scale medevac.

**The Centurion**- The British tank, made its debut during the Korean War due to its excellent performance in the hilly and mountain terrain of the country. These tanks taught us that anywhere a tank can go, is tank country: even the tops of Korean mountains", showing the Centurions proved to be very mobile in the Korean terrain.

**Super Bazooka-** Is the common name for a man-portable recoilless anti-tank rocket launcher weapon, widely fielded by the United States Army. Also referred to as the Stovepipe. The innovative bazooka was among the first generation of rocket-propelled anti-tank weapons used in infantry combat. It was deadly effective against dug-in troops, as a short-range anti-pillbox and anti-personnel weapon. They were also effective against mobile machine gun and mortar crews who moved forward with the second assault

**The Sabre-** The first Jet-versus-Jet Dogfight was basically fought in the area called the MiG Alley. The primary fights were between the American Sabre F-86 and the Soviet MiG-15. The first combat record in Korea was, by any standards, impressive. Of the 900 aerial victories claimed by USAF pilots during the war, 792 were MiG-15s shot down by Sabre. The MiG-15s in their turn managed to knock down only 78 Sabre. American fighter pilots thus established a ten-to-one kill/loss ratio in their favor.

**Sikorsky H-19-** A sweeping deployment of the Sikorsky Helicopters worked closely with Mobile Army Surgical Hospitals (MASH) soldiers. They would fly into dangerous enemy areas with the purpose of replenishing supplies and carry out the wounded. Working with the **MASH** unit, they were responsible in saving many of our wounded., they saved many of our young veterans. (Wikipedia)

# VIETNAM WAR

## Voice of Humanity

I chose the following poems that are perhaps known to most Vietnam Vets but not so much by civilians.

1. *Yea though I walk through the valley of the shadow of death I will fear no evil,*
   *For I am the evilest son of a bitch in the valley.*

2. *We the unwilling*
   *Led by the unqualified*
   *Die for the ungrateful*
   (This poem was written on the back of a Zippo lighter)
   *Author Paul Warren: copyright Paul Warren*

   *We have done so much*
   *with so little*
   *for so long*
   *Now we can do anything with nothing.*
   *(Seen on the roof of a building between Pleiku and Nha Trang from a helicopter.)*

# CHAPTER 21

*American Life in the 1960's -70's*

Not only was the war in Vietnam crazy but so was America at the time. The times were changing. There were still families who followed the 50's traditions such as the man being the sole financial supporter of the family and the woman was the stay at home wife and mother. They still believed in their middle-class values such as, belief in God, hard work, and the service to their country. They were still watching the Andy Griffith Show and The Beverly Hillbillies. But as world information was made clearer every day, with the use of satellite communication, long distance telephone abilities and the television in our living rooms, life in the 60's was indeed changing.

The Vietnam War could visit us in our very living room. So, we could see the battles and the killings of our children. We began seeing the protest against the war. We could also witness the civil rights protests for the rights of Black Americans, women fighting for equality and the Gay Rights Movement. It just wasn't the naive innocent American citizen anymore. The world became smaller, with world communication at our fingertips along with protest music and art becoming more available to all, it was a definite time of change.

With the introduction of the birth control pill sexuality became more open. Tie dye shirts, bell bottom jeans, braless women, and long hair or Afros on young men and women became the attire for the young. Music was the genre for teenage rebellion. As the young fought for change, the family values began to change. The youth of our country revolted against the materialism and the mainstream of the times. They were a "counterculture" that started a social revolution throughout our country. They were against the guidelines of the fifties and the US extensive military intervention in Vietnam. They called themselves "Hippies" and fought toward liberation in our society for equality for all minorities, sexual freedoms and they questioned the authority and government. As folk singer Bob Dylan wrote "The Times They Are a-Changing". The times did change, and things have never been the same.

## The Very Confused Vietnam War

So, we have "The War to End All Wars" which was the catalyst to "The Good War" which was the reason for "The Forgotten War" and now we have Vietnam.

We fought In WWI because we were attacked, in WWII we were attacked, and in Korea, we had made a promise. But there was no world war and no promise made in the Vietnam War. So, why did we send our children to fight in this war? Some say it was to stop the spread of communism, some say it had to do with political legacies, points of view, some say it was greed, some say it was a proxy between the United States and the Soviet Union. Proxies means someone else's yard beside their own. The reason was to fight communism vs. capitalism/democracy between Soviet Union and America.

Since some people believe it was to curb communism, some believe it was unjust, some will talk about political legacies, some say it was used as a proxy. I will leave it up to you as to why we went to war.

The following are two versions of the war, along with the veteran's stories as they recall.

### Version One

We have been involved with Vietnam from 1945-1975.The total purpose was to stop the spread of communism in Vietnam. So, when the French asked for our support President Truman increased our involvement by giving financial and military assistance to the French forces fighting in Vietnam. We believed we had to restrict the communist domination otherwise it would lead to a change of balance in Southeast Asia and our major security interests in the world would be disturbed. We also began sending troops not for combat but to supervise the U.S. military equipment that was supporting the French. Then under President Eisenhower comes the Geneva Convention which poses a temporary division of Vietnam with a nationwide election to take place in 1956. Even before the due date for the election North Vietnam reneges on the agreement. We begin deploying the Military Assistance Group which marked the official beginning of our involvement in the Vietnam War. It was six or seven years later, under President Kennedy that we used herbicidal warfare. U.S. planes continued spraying herbicides and defoliants over South Vietnam until 1971. He also stated our purpose was to prevent communist domination of South Vietnam. It was when we were said to have been attacked in the Gulf of Tonkin that President Johnson escalated the war. We sent large numbers of troops into Vietnam for the first time under President Johnson. He expanded the numbers in 1966. Then came President Richard Nixon who began reducing the amount of our troops in 1969-74 which was called Vietnamization. It was in 1975 that we left Vietnam, the first war we ever lost with 58,000 of our young soldiers' dead.

What do you think so far?

Just asking

## Version Two

In the beginning President Wilson (1913-1921) ignored Ho Chi Minh's petition to help create an independent Vietnam and then when President Roosevelt took office, (1933-45) he declined requests from the French to help re-organize Vietnam. So far, so good. We said no to both lead parties. But when President Truman took office (1945-53) and France mentioned if we did not back them, they might have to go to different world leaders for help, he agreed. We sent both financial and military support for the French fighting the Vietnamese.

The problem was that during WWII many promises were made for the support to Vietnam. It was in 1946 Ho Chi Minh wrote a letter to President Truman. He stated "From 1941 to 1945 we fought bitterly, sustained by the patriotism of our fellow- countrymen and by the promise made by the Allies. What we ask has already been granted to the Philippines. Like the Philippines our goal is full independence and full cooperation with the United States. We will do our best to make this independence and cooperation profitable to the whole world" The letter for some reason never reached the president.

What Happened to the letter?

Just asking

Not many know that Ho Chi Minh lived in America for more than thirty years. He believed in a lot of what our democracy stood for and when in 1945 he became leader of Vietnam, his speech was that of his favorite US president, Thomas Jefferson. That was then and this is now and Vietnam is a communist country.

Why the change?

Just asking

In 1971 when the Pentagon papers were made public, they revealed that the United States had expanded its war with the bombing of Cambodia and Laos, coastal raids on North Vietnam, and Marine Corps attacks, none of which had been reported by the American media. The most damaging revelations in the papers revealed that four administrations (Truman, Eisenhower, Kennedy, and Johnson), had misled the public regarding their intentions. For example, the Eisenhower administration actively worked against the Geneva Accords which was what Ho Chi Minh was talking about in his lost letter. John F. Kennedy had experienced a few failures like "The Bay of Pigs and "The building of the Berlin Wall" and was looking for a way to reassure our power credibility as world leader and he felt Vietnam would be the place. He sent a reconnaissance mission to fly over Vietnam and see what the situation was and if we should become more involved. The answer was no, we should not get more involved. So, we got more involved and

President Kennedy sent 16,000 more troops before his death. It was during his 1964 presidential campaign President Johnson had decided to expand the war including plans to bomb North Vietnam well before the 1964 Election. He had been outspoken against doing so during the election and claimed that his opponent Barry Goldwater was the one who wanted to bomb North Vietnam. Barry Goldwater responded with "Johnson kept reiterating that he would never send our boys to fight but at the same time he knew he was going to. I knew ten days before he sent them." Johnson lied about the attack on us by the North Vietnamese in the Gulf of Tonkin which escalated the war even further.

There was a thought that no American President wanted to be the first to lose a war and many of our children died for their arrogance.

In another example, a memo from the Defense Department under the Johnson Administration listed the reasons for American persistence:

70% – To avoid a humiliating U.S. defeat (to our reputation as a guarantor).
20% – To keep [South Vietnam] (and the adjacent) territory from Chinese hands.
10% – To permit the people [of South Vietnam] to enjoy a better, freer way of life.
ALSO – To emerge from the crisis without unacceptable taint from methods used.
NOT – To help a friend, although it would be hard to stay in if asked out.

Now what do you think? Could the truth be in both?

Just asking

The price for all these reasons has cost us more than 58,000 young people who died, along with those who came home with physical and emotional crises. They also came home with war protesters blaming them for a war and others blaming them for losing the war. These young people who were drafted, those who were doing their commitment to their country, those just trying for the GI Bill, are not the ones that make political decisions or lie to the public. They were the ones who came back to a place where they were hated, called losers, chastised by society and ended up with a great deal of their lives wasted. Someone once told me that you never leave a war. It is in your mind, your dreams, and your soul until you die.

Where should the blame be laid?

Just asking

# AS THEY REMEMBER

# CHAPTER 22

*Major General Wayne Jackson*
*Heritage Scottish/Norwegian - Army*

It was truly my good fortunate meeting this man. Call it luck, serendipity or karma. But not only did he give time for his interview but set up a time that I might interview five other veterans, in the area, who had served. They included veterans from WWII, Korea and Vietnam.

He explained that most of his service was in intelligence so not sure what he might be able to share, but would help in any way possible.

I explained the three sections of questions and he was onboard. So, we began.

"I had a very quick childhood," he said, "my whole life has pretty much been in structured environments. I was in a boy's home with very focused schedules. I was in the Boy Scouts and an Eagle Scout with high moral codes and a belief in one's country, and responsibility for it.

"When my dad got re-married, I went to live with him and his new wife. I realized right away she never had kids of her own, and was very used to a white rug kind of setting. She was not ready for a teenage football player like me who brought his teenage testosterone into such a neat quiet environment. I decided the best move for me was to direct myself to my future.

"I was looking for a direction and found out the military had a plan. If I joined the service, I would be eligible for the GI Bill which would be my road to a good education. I needed to quit school in order to join, the reason being, I would get in just under the wire before the bill would be dropped. I joined three months before that happened. I had learned at a very young age that if it is to be it is up to me and so I joined and never looked back.

"It was a quirk of fate that I scored high on tests that ended me in a school for cryptology. I was told after training I would be heading to Alaska, but not to worry since there are girls behind every tree. Just FYI there were no trees in Alaska just a place where you can go lose your mind if you're not careful. That is exactly what happened to my commanding officer. Because of the Top Secret Crypto clearance we would be locked in a small room, just the two of us. You have to be there to understand the isolation of miles of nothing outside but cold, polar bears and penguins. Inside you had your equipment and one other person in the room with you. The Sergeant did have a break with reality and needed some rest and relaxation time. Because of this I became at 17 years old Staff Sergeant and it was because of the Top Secret Crypto clearance that my life just went forward in the military.

"From that one little quirk of fate I went on for more military education which included the basic and advanced officer courses at Signal and Military Intelligence Schools along with graduating from the US Army Command and General Staff College and the US Army War College. Because of this training I was able to serve in various overseas theaters of operation and hence commanded Signal Corps, Military Intelligence and Civil Affairs. I also served as Director of Counter Intelligence and Security.

He stopped and said, "This might sound a bit boring to you but what I cannot tell was very important exciting and I was proud to be a part of it. So enough about bragging, except for one more. I was able to swear my own son into the service and it was one of my proudest moments."

Tell a bit about after the service?

"My wife Lahoma, who I met while we were both attending college, and I are now living in Florida. Our children are grown and happy and we are enjoying the warm weather. But as far as retirement, I never use that word. At present I am involved in a program that works with wounded veterans.

"This program is a bit different than the ones like the 'Wounded Warriors'. We take the wounded warriors out for therapeutic activities that are supportive and encouraging. We realized that each warrior needed a case manager, a family. This program invites the warrior case manager and family for a free week to a program in Florida. There are no requirements to participate since we believe these veterans have had enough scheduled appointments and activities. We do have an array of opportunities like deep sea fishing, relaxation with a cool breeze and light lunch on the beach and many family events. It is up to the warrior to decide and choose. First step in empowerment and independence. I love the work."

I asked for any last-minute statements and he said. "Sure,

1. We are all guaranteed creation to cremation and no one gets out.
2. If it is to be, it is up to me. If more young people believed that, I think they would try harder."

## Questions

1. Why do we have wars?
   "There are the haves and have nots."
2. What was the media like?
   "Be careful of what you say. They can misinterpret. In other words, cover your ass."
3. What was the role of women?
   "I think what is happening now is not bad. They did have to change a couple of routines so that women could pass boot camp. One example is the pull up bar. If women want to join, they should be allowed."
4. How were gays treated?
   "They were there, but most just left alone."
5. What would you tell young people today?
   "The discipline, purpose, commitment to something is important and I think some young people are missing that. The service just might be the right place for them to be."
6. Would you do it again?
   He tipped back his head and with a slight grin said,
   "Never doubt it."

# CHAPTER 23

## *"Ghost" John Hourihan – Heritage Irish/French – Army*

### Life Before the War

I met Johnny about 73 years ago when my mother brought him home from the hospital. He is my younger brother and the first boy born into the then family of five children, with two more named Neil and Dennis appearing in the next four years. My brother completed three tours of duty in the Vietnam War as a linguist, a total of about 34 months. He was awarded the National Defense ribbon, The Vietnam Service ribbon with five campaign stars, and the Cross of Gallantry for valor in the face of the enemy. His unit was awarded the Congressional and Presidential unit citations.

I asked him if he would be willing to be interviewed by me. He agreed and we went to the Hopedale Town Park with a couple cups of coffee, sat in the sunny sand at the edge of the pond and began.

My first question was, could you tell, from your perspective, a bit about your childhood?

He said, "I guess I felt my first real home was a five-room house on six acres of land in rural Massachusetts. It wasn't really large enough for nine people, but it was an idyllic wilderness for a kid my age, four. There were fields of apple trees, woods filled with grapes, blueberries, black raspberries. There were wild rabbits and pheasants in the back of the house and a subsistence garden in the front yard. ... There was Butch the cat, a pet squirrel that I trained to eat out of my hand, and Sea Bee my dog, a black and white Springer spaniel.

I asked what kind of games they played in the fifties and he said, "Snow angels, sledding, shoe skating in the winter. In the summer it was all baseball, and going with my friends Spike, Danny and Robbie to shoot our BB guns out in the woods. In the house, we watched a black and white TV with a broken horizontal hold, listened to my mother read all the classics to us, and during Lent she would have us sit around her and say the rosary. Most importantly was the amazing thrill of just being alive in such an unencumbered world that made so much sense to me."

Would you talk a bit about your parents?

"My dad worked in a shoe factory, tried to usher in a union. Accomplished it and then got black-balled by the industry for years. It was then that we learned what poverty was, and hunger. He would stand us kids, all seven of us, in front of him and lecture us on the plight of the common man. He would talk to us about the importance of keeping your word, and also knowing the importance of being Irish. He was our social conscience, and I loved him despite his need for drink."

What about your mother?

"My mother was the smartest kid in the high school. The nuns told me that. She married my dad, had seven children, made sure we followed the ten commandments, made sure we knew we were loved, and always made sure we had Christmas. She worked nights at a hat factory, came home and made our lunches for school, made supper for the night and then started washing the laundry in the bath tub. She then got up at six a.m. She woke, fed us, and got us off to school. She then sat down at the kitchen table and had herself a cup of tea."

Can you tell a bit about school?

Johnny starts with, "My problem with school was that I did not want to go. First, I loved my world in the country. Second, I had a patch over my lazy eye, my first set of teeth had all broken due to a fall down a flight of stairs and the dentist said, 'Don't pull them, he needs to keep the root spaces until the next set of teeth starts coming in.' So I started my first day with a patch over my eye, black fang teeth in my mouth, and a patch of hair missing from my head. I just hated it, I not only scared the other kids, but I think the nuns were a little nervous. I'm pretty sure they thought I was possessed."

I asked about his school years.

He replied, "When I was in the fifth grade or so we had to move to Arizona because my younger brother had asthma. So new school begins. It was different there. Grownups had six-guns in their holsters just like the Lone Ranger, kids had fist fights, knife fights, and I learned I had to do the same. We lived in a barrio next to a junkyard. I had learned to fight from my dad, but I also learned I could scare the crap out of anyone by just starting with screaming, punching, biting, scratching and kicking. I figured out then that there were no rules in fighting except to win. They had no idea what I would do next and that was my power. After beating them one at a time they began chasing me in a pack. That is when Rosie and I became friends. Rosie was a very large Mexican kid and that ended the bullying. I believe I was bullied because I was the new kid and I was small. It was there and then that I learned about the injustice of the world."

How long did you stay in Arizona?

"It was about two years. My brother was doing well, and my parents decided we were to head home. I was so excited to be going home to all my friends and I thought, our home in the country. ... We arrived and I couldn't wait to find my old friends. But what I found was they were the same, but I wasn't. I had become someone who was filled with anger that had begun with my leaving my paradise in the country, continued being built through my father's ordeals and demons that so directly flowed downhill to the rest of us, along with the Arizona experience. I was filled with anger. ... Now it was back to Grammar School to what I thought was to the comfortable innocence at St Mary's protected by God, my family and a circle of friends who I no longer knew, or rather who no longer knew me."

I asked how he ended up in the Army.

"Simple," he said. "After high school I did a year of college and then was beginning my second year. My dreams were pretty much nothing other than not working in a shoe factory like my old man. So, one day I went home, saw that my father had come in with his belligerent, arrogant, abusive, drunken personality and I decided to put an end to my present way of life. I went to join the Air Force. The recruiter was out to lunch so I joined the Army. I was eighteen when I signed and went in on my 19th birthday.

"The first days were a blur of people screaming at me for no apparent reason, and a lot of stupid teenagers who thought they had just become John Wayne and others who were so pissed they got drafted that they started fights with anything that moved. I made friends with the biggest guy in the company (a trick I learned in school). Frank James was 6'7" and black from the streets of Newark, N.J. He was smart and tough. It was there in basic training that I learned that we had a war going on. James told me."

Tell me about basic training.

John said, "Basic training was hell. I got pneumonia, but I kept going, did well and got an early promotion. I was then sent to the DLIWC (Defense Language Institute West Coast) where I learned the Vietnamese language, and it was where I found out that I was going to that war.

"I was signed up for the Army Security Agency (think NSA in uniform) I was trained in the methods of intercepting enemy radio transmissions and translating them. I also was trained in firing an M-14 (sharpshooter)."

Where did your training take place?

"It started in Monterey, California, where my time was split between going to the beach and chasing women. When I went to San Angelo, Texas where I dated a nurse, sang at the Gas Light lounge at the Ramada Inn, drank a lot, and learned about the R-390 radio that I would be using to intercept enemy transmissions The first time I heard a taped Viet Cong transmission in a classroom in Texas with a hangover, was the first time I knew I was in trouble."

## Life During the War

"Three years out of high school I was learning things I never would have learned in Hopedale, Milford or even Phoenix. The truth of war is different when you are in the middle of it. The only real protection you have is yourself and God's will. You either accept that or you go crazy.

"I was in a country where Thieu and Ky had been elected president and vice president in a farce election where anyone who wanted peace wasn't allowed to run, and the winners only got thirty-five percent of the vote. Any kid brought up in Milford would have smelled a fix, but my problem was deeper than worrying about politics, or war and peace, or who was right or wrong. I was more interested in keeping myself alive.

"It was more than two years since I had first arrived in country, and my attitude toward what was happening in me had – grown up. I was no longer a nineteen-year-old child who didn't know his country was at war. The smell of gunpowder, the heart-thumping pound of the sound of a helicopter, the sleepless periods, the ghosts of dead friends, explosions, small arms fire, the heavy smell of the red clay plateaus, the stink of nuoc mam fish sauce and the skunk-cabbage stench of ba-moui-ba beer, it all was forever embedded in me. I was a thousand years old and I finally knew who I was. I was the guy in charge of me."

Asked about the environment he worked in.

He said, "On a good day, our operations compound was located in a concertina wire enclosure. There were five deuce-an-a-half trucks backed up to each side of a raised ramp and a walkway that was even with the back doors of the trucks. Inside each cubicle were six radio and tape recorder positions. Three on each side. Although there were windows behind us it was still hot even when they were opened. We sat and listened and taped everything. What we didn't translate in the day we translated in the night when there wasn't a lot of radio traffic. This was Pleiku. It was a nasty existence, but it was the best situation of my time in Vietnam.

"Pleiku was in the central highlands. It was a town on a plateau of red clay by day, and by night it was a firestorm of mortars, rockets and flares lighting up the land and the Spooky gunships lighting up the sky with mini-guns burping out red tracer rounds. Often we would be hit with mortars, small arms or rockets, and we'd hustle to our alert positions around the perimeter of our company and wait. My position for a while was in a ditch about three feet deep. During the rainy season (about six months of every year) it would fill with water and we would sit in the water up to our chests and watch for snakes. I spent 34 months in Vietnam and was stationed in Pleiku, Phu Bai, Chu Lai, Da Nang, An My, Tan Son Nhut, Phan Thiet, Nha Trang, Phan Rang, Cam Ranh, Cong Mountain, Dragon Mountain, several LZs and a month flying on C-130s and 123s all over the country carrying classified material among Radio Research outfits, which is what they called the Army Security Agency people there since it was supposedly against the Geneva Convention for us to be there. I don't know why. It was during this time on the planes that I somehow got the nick name "The Ghost." I guess it was because I kept showing up for a few minutes and then leaving, but it stuck until I left the service."

What about the people of Vietnam?

"There was a part of Vietnam service that no one who hadn't been there would ever understand. It was that once we had met the people of South Vietnam, heard how they called Ho Chi Minh affectionately Uncle Ho, a lot of us didn't feel the government had made the right choice sending us here, but we felt we owed something to our country. These were the rules, so we showed up and stayed. I met a lot of Vietnamese people, and this is why I decided I was no longer shooting people. I turned in my M-14 and decided that I would only go by other people's rules if they didn't contradict what was right, but for now, I was here. I knew there would be repercussions for not carrying a gun. I also knew that I had a Top Secret Crypto clearance and was one of the best linguists they had and that might keep me out of any real strict punishment.

"Just about now is when I thought I was becoming paranoid, like someone was always watching me. I felt it was because I would not carry a weapon. I wasn't paranoid it turned out. It was just a heightened awareness as told to me by some officers who even admitted they were involved. It seems that there were a lot of bets on whether or not I could be 'talked into' asking for, or better still, begging for a weapon. Some career Army NCOs and officers seemed insulted that I would turn in my weapon and not ask to leave the country. So it became a concerted effort to make me do just that, beg for a gun or ask to go home. The longer I avoided what they wanted, the more they saw me as 'winning.'

I had to be very careful because no one plays nice when they are losing. But as Woody Guthrie and Scrapper Jack Hourihan said, 'Deal me your hardest hand and I'll win this Goddamn game.' That's how I felt at the time – arrogant and angry."

I asked what were his intentions when joining the Army.

He said, "By now I had tossed out the thirty years of service idea and was content that the government would pay my way through school if I just earned my money, did my job as a linguist, stayed out of jail, and got an honorable discharge."

## Life After the War

"At the age where most people step out of college and begin their adult life, I stepped out of one war and right into another. The anger that began to fill me wasn't left over from the war as everyone thought. The anger was because of the latent hatred I had faced since I had returned. This new world was in so many ways more hostile, hateful, and deceiving than anything a war can manufacture. It quickly became clear that, for the most part, the America I had returned to wouldn't have cared all that much if I had died.

"The stability I had hoped would welcome me back, the warmth of a grateful country or the stabilizing cement of a loving family didn't exist. Added to that, I was an alcoholic, pot head, anger stuffed, paranoid, twenty something who had spent too many years in a war. To me, Vietnam had been a mystical war. No one had survived. We all died in Vietnam. Some of us came back to life dead. If you can't understand that, you weren't part of that war.

"About a month after I got out, I got a letter from the NSA wanting to know if I wanted a job. I lit it on fire and lit a joint with it.

"One lonely night, half drunk, on a stoop in front of the Co-Mac bar, and hypnotized by the sight of my own breath in the frigid air, I was approached by an old friend. Wally had returned a year before me. He sat down beside me on the cement step silent as an angel in the fog. 'You have to get out of here,' he slurred. 'What?' 'If you don't get out of here you are going to end up like me.'

"'Heroin,' he said. 'After a while it's the only thing that works.' He paused, then added, "They hate us, you know.' He nodded toward the cars passing by on the Main Street of the town where we started together in first grade. 'We embarrass them.'

"I had come from an inner-city tenement, through the hunger of rural Massachusetts, past the violent poverty of a South Phoenix barrio, into the pompous reality of a white Anglo-Saxon Protestant small town, and through the filth of the Vietnam War. I found myself jumping when a car backfired, jumping when its horn blared, jumping when fireworks went off. I realized right then and there I had to make some changes. I did.

"Before I knew it, I had married and had two very beautiful kids. I began working as an editor in a local newspaper. Then I was hired to develop and implement a newspaper in Laconia, New Hampshire. I then ended up at the Connecticut Post and earned fifteen awards for my column, including state, regional and national ones, but by that time my kids had grown and my wife and I had been divorced.

"I am married now to a woman I have known since she was fourteen. Her name is Lin and she is the love of my life. We became closer to ourselves to each other and to nature. We stopped trying to 'move up', got off the ladder and returned to the values we had grown up with. I ended up retired due to the effects of Agent Orange; diabetes, heart trouble and yes, PTSD."

## Questions

1. Why do we have wars?

   "I wonder about this a lot since I came back. I think we have wars mostly because humans like to kill stuff. There are all the political, financial, geographical and religious arguments for and against it, and we always have a reason for believing we must go to war: The godless Indians, the godless Japanese, the godless

Huns. Well, everyone is a godless something or other. Or we scare everyone with lies like the Gulf of Tonkin, or WMDs, and now that the leader of North Korea is insane we can't let him launch his nukes at us, or the godless Iranians need to be put in their place. But when it comes right down to it, we wouldn't send our kids or go ourselves if we didn't like to kill stuff. Since just about anyone you ask who has been to a war will say, war never solves anything, the only reason I can think of is that we just like the thrill of hunting something down and killing it or them. I spent thirty-four months in Vietnam. Somewhere in the middle I made a decision. I would die for my country, but I would no longer kill for my country. With a year left, I returned my automatic M-14, told my Executive Officer I would not go home, I would not ask for another duty, I would continue to do my job of finding and reporting the whereabouts of enemy troops, (and believe me I was sent to every hot spot in the country, even to a Special Forces unit) but I wouldn't carry a weapon any more. I figured the information that I provided to others about the whereabouts of the enemy could be used in many ways, and how it was used was up to them."

2. What was the role of black soldiers?

   "There was still a lot of racism in the Army. However, in my outfit, where the average education of the rank and file was between two and three years of college, there was much less outward racism. We had a black officer, and black NCOs who supervised white soldiers, and they were as respected as anyone else. The longer a person spent in the war zone the less racism he could harbor. Your life depended on the other guys and what color their skin was really didn't matter. We used to say, 'We're all green now.'"

   A friend of mine, George Duggins, who later became the president of the Vietnam Veterans of America, and I had long conversations about how young black men felt fighting in Vietnam. It was George who told me Mohammed Ali's great quote, "No Viet Cong ever called me nigger." Racism was still there, but we were dealing with it. George died from the effects of Agent Orange. It was the first time I cried since I got home.

3. What was the treatment for PTSD?

"I don't remember PTSD being part of the vernacular, but I knew that as I put more and more time in country, my senses became extremely alive. Loud noises, flashes of light, and vast spaces such as open fields seemed to have a detrimental effect on my wellbeing. Imagine coming back to a world where this was bothering you and you were now experiencing loud noises from cars and trucks, loud music, the flash of sunlight off chrome and endless windows reflecting sunlight, and anger that was not because of the war but because of the horrendous treatment you received from the people in your own country, people you supposedly had been fighting for. This wasn't treated. It was barely acknowledged as anything but 'those crazy Vietnam vets.' PTSD probably cost me my first marriage."

4. How were women treated and what was their role?

"Women were nurses, donut dollies, or Vietnamese women. The first two were treated with respect. The third type of women we met were the ones who worked for us or the ones who were hookers downtown. I worry now every time I meet a Vietnamese woman here in the states. Even though I tried to be a good person while I was there, I almost want to apologize. We treated the Vietnamese badly. Once I was traveling through Da Nang on my way up country. Heading for the airport I grabbed a ride with a Catholic chaplain in a Jeep. Subsequently, he stopped and picked up two young black soldiers. They began talking to each other and kept referring to the Vietnamese as 'zips' and 'gooks' and 'slant eyes.' They were words we all used. After a few miles, the chaplain asked, 'Is that what you n.....s call the Vietnamese?' The two kids were so embarrassed. They apologized and asked to get out, but we all laughed nervously, me because both of these guys had loaded guns and were sitting behind me and were probably pretty pissed off, but everyone learned a lesson and we drove them to their outfit. We were all just kids in a really rotten situation."

5. How were gay and lesbian soldiers treated?
"Terrible Tubby Johnson was a staff sergeant, and was respected by all of the guys who worked for him. One night he went to one of the NCO clubs on Artillery Hill, half a mile away from our company area, and came back beaten pretty badly. It was because he was gay. I would like to go on record now telling those who did it, this is why your pet boa constrictor company mascot ended up dead with his head cut off and stuck on a stake outside your orderly room. There were a lot of people who were pretty upset that you decided to beat a man you had outnumbered just for the way he was born. He was also born smart, tough, and a great person, and was awarded a Bronze Star for his bravery. You missed that."

6. What was the role of the media?
"Our media was Johnny Grant in Saigon on the radio (Adrian Cronaur had just left when I got here in Feb. of 67) and word of mouth. Then there was Stars and Stripes (the Army newspaper). Both the radio and the newspaper were censored. But the news you heard at home was also not quite true. On the night before I went home on my first leave from Pleiku, a sniper found his way into our water tower. He got off a few shots and everyone took cover. A Royal Hawaiian buck sergeant who was upset, commandeered the APC and drove up to the tower. He shot the sniper and we went on with life. A few days later I arrived home in Hopedale, Mass. on a thirty-day leave. While I watched, the TV news told everyone how a Radio Research Company had been attacked by a company of Viet Cong and after a 'pitched battle' the communists were driven off by 'an armored force.' We tend to glorify wars."

7. What would you tell young people today about joining the service?
"I believe service is good for young people. I do think, however, that they should have the option of service that doesn't include killing people. Sort of like the Peace Corp or VISTA."

# CHAPTER 24

*"My Men First" Sam A. Martin - Heritage Irish - Army*

## Life Before War

Sam was old school. He spoke with a very soft tone, was polite to all, and I never heard him raise his voice. He stood about five-eleven, with his back straight like a soldier still at attention. His expression told so little that it was impossible to read him at first. In time, as we worked together, I found him to be a man of integrity showing wisdom in his actions, and respect for those we worked for. Those we worked for were the Vietnam veterans.

It was about two years later that we really sat down to an interview. It was worth the wait. I told Sam that I start interviews with who he was before he entered the service. So, hopefully the reader will get to know the person before he enters the war, and his words will be read with feeling and not just facts from a book.

So, we start with Sam's younger days and I ask him a bit about family. He begins, "Since extended families were part of life in the forties and fifties and ours was no exception. We lived in a huge, very old Elizabethan style house. It was a blue collar semi-industrial town and with a very extended family. Our family included myself, my two brothers, my mom, my dad, my grandmother, a great grandmother and a great uncle. We were not a very religious family. We did try the Catholic, Congregational and Episcopalian churches but it was pretty much going through the motions."

Tell me a little about your parents?

"Before marriage my mother had a career as a nurse. After marriage, she began running the household. How she did it I will never know. She took care of everyone, along with the meals, washing cloths and doing house work. She also made our clothes from school shirts to pajamas. I guess the term for how she managed was patience." He went on to say, "My mother was a strong woman. She was tolerant, calm, wise and generous. She was raised an orphan and yet was able to give greatly to others and asked nothing in return. She envied no one and she coveted nothing. She became ill and that illness lasted for eight years. Much of what I just told you was in her eulogy given by my older brother."

When asked about his dad he replied, "Without hesitation, complaint or rancor, he took care of my mother. He never gave up. My brothers and I learned about duty and honesty and tolerance and responsibility and love from our dad. His work was that of a banker. He would religiously take the train to Boston every day. Those were the days you stayed with a company for the duration of your working life. My dad was no exception. He worked 42 years for National Shawmut Bank. However, the family suffered as we never shared a closeness with each other. We never discussed emotions or ideas or futures. Work seemed to be the most important and it came first."

I have known Sam for a few years now. I wondered if he knows just how wise his mother was in that she instilled through example. She reminds me of a saying I heard once, "To do for the sake of it. It will become the reward." His mother instilled in him patience, tolerance and wisdom. I see it in him when we worked together and now sitting for this interview.

I also believe his father instilled honesty, responsibility and courage. This I believe you will see when he talks about his time in Vietnam.

As far as childhood went Sam said, "My folks were depression-era people, and so the family motto was save- save- save and so we did. We did the things that all kids did for money back then. We mowed lawns, shoveled snow, delivered newspapers, sold magazines and at Christmas we sold candles and cards." The next thing he said, took me by surprise "It was in the fourth grade that I really found my niche. We moved into a house that was adjacent to the first hole of the Bellevue Golf Club. At the age of ten I took part in a robust caddy program as a rookie. I fell in love with my caddying and with the game of golf, even with the pay at a dollar for nine holes and three dollars for eighteen." I mentioned to him that it usually takes a bit longer for a person to reach his or her level of satisfaction in the job world. But here's Sam at ten and quite proud of himself.

As far as school went, he said, "My dad did not feel average was good enough for college, so, off to a Naval Honor School. Tabor was an all-boys school where we wore naval uniforms the better part of the academic year. Not only was this environment new to me but it was also decided I would stay back a year. Not having any say about this move myself, I was losing all my friends including my first girlfriend. I believe being so embarrassed about staying back, losing all friends, and feeling all alone caused me to take comfort in becoming a loner. I expect this secondary school experience also contributed to a relatively low self- esteem.

My college years were a bit of a challenge. I had such difficulty with the atmosphere," he said. "After four years at an all-boys school, I was extremely shy around the opposite sex. No meaningful relationships happened during those four years. But, my second love, after golf, did happen in college. I received a scholarship to study at the University in Oslo Norway. That trip marked the beginning of a love affair that has never ended. It is called international business. When I heard that the credits, I received from Oslo University would be accepted from Rollin College and I was eligible to graduate. I couldn't wait."

Why did you join the service with a war exploding in Vietnam?

This handsome quiet guy with poor self-esteem says, "Quite frankly, at this point I was tired of going to school and as I like to say the military obligation is like paying rent for living in the USA, so I see it as part of life's process." On April 1, 1967, he entered the United States Army.

## Life During the War

Tell me about your entrance into the Army?

He began with, "Well, due to my love of dogs I had wanted to be a scout dog platoon leader, but no such luck. As a newly minted "Butter Bar" (rookie second lieutenant) I found myself driving north to Washington, D.C. Due to my height and weight I became a candidate for the third infantry, commonly referred as the Old Guard. This organization was responsible for the security of Washington. Due to the recent assassination of Martin Luther King, the Old Guard was deployed throughout Washington to curb the burning of a large segment of the city. I had to jump right in not really knowing what I should be doing. It was the 1968 riots, and I took over a platoon as part of the 3rd Infantry, Old Guard. I was given a section of Washington, DC (predominately black section) to patrol and keep secure from looters.

Aside from security the Old Guard was responsible for The Tomb of the Unknown Soldier, foreign Heads of State arrivals and departures, Pentagon tours and Medal of Honor ceremonies were all part of our daily routine. During my tour I also participated in the Nixon presidential inauguration and the funeral of Robert Kennedy at the Arlington National Cemetery.

We also did as many as eight to ten funerals per day, the majority of which were soldiers killed in Vietnam. So, we started to bury veterans from Vietnam before we even got there. Not a good way to start your military experience.

We all knew our next tour was coming up and we all knew it would be Vietnam. The war, at that time, was pretty much at its height and we were living life to its fullest knowing that some of us might not return home. We knew this simply by counting the eight out of ten we buried every day.

Getting ready for Vietnam I was assigned three weeks of jungle school in the Republic of Panama, good place to get used to the heat that we would experience in Vietnam. Not only was the heat miserable but the ants seemed to like us a lot." After three whole weeks in a jungle these guys are ready to go to war. Right!

Sam said, "I then got transferred to Travis AFB in California to await my flight to Vietnam. When we landed, to this day, I can still remember the smell. It smelled of bombs, mud, and rice. It just stunk.

The soldiers waiting for us to get off the plane so they can get on and go home were the weariest of soldiers. Their faces were drawn and exhausted, their uniforms were faded and wasted, and they just looked so worn out, and old, and somehow empty. I really don't know how to explain what I was feeling just at that moment. I was scared and depressed. All I could think about was three hundred and sixty-five days to go and looking at those soldiers just made me wonder what they had gone through."

Sam would know soon enough just what those soldiers went through because after seeing those worn out soldiers, he was assigned to the Mobile River Forces,9th Infantry Division located one hundred miles south of Saigon in the various Mekong Delta tributaries within this region.

Sam went on to explain the area, "The "Delta" as it was called was the 'bread-basket' of Vietnam. It was a large, wet, flat area that produced a major portion of the rice grown in Vietnam. We, the Mobile Riverine Force were a joint venture between the US Navy and the US Army. We lived on boats stationed on the major rivers and we were inserted for combat operations either by boats and/or helicopters. Our basic operations were four days in the field and one day on the boat."

When I asked about the environment Sam said, "From the looks of the area I knew I would become a swamp rat by the time I got through. Nothing but water, water and more water. The wet geography led to immersion foot, ring worm, rickets, leaches and other skin complications. Bad feet became one of the major reasons soldiers were unable to continually go into the field. It was also one of the reasons that we rarely had a full platoon. I some time had only half a platoon to go into battle with."

How do you handle the tension during these times?

He said, "Sometimes it is just the stress of waiting or the tension you hold in while you wait. For example, we'll be listening to the radio and Hanoi Hanna comes on and announced that my ship the LST (landing ship tanks) is supposed to be blown up tomorrow?" Sam added, "that would make quite a bang and lots of fireworks since we supply two brigades with all their ammunition." That is what a knot in your stomach or sweat on your brow is all about, along with writing a letter home that you feel could be the last. "False information. We were not blown up."

So, no fake news now. Sam continued with, "We were called in as a ready reaction force for a sister company in heavy contact with a large VC battalion. We were quickly air-lifted off the ship's flight deck and joined the contact late that afternoon. The helicopter needed to get in and out of the area as fast as it could. So, they would hover over an open area and we would jump six feet sometimes eight. We would land in the open field with either mud to greet us or rock-solid ground, along with gunfire at times. We then headed for cover into the jungle. That is where we re-group and start supporting our sister company. The contact was intense with air strikes, artillery and helicopter firing, along with gunships supporting our ground efforts. This is where I was wounded. It was in my right arm and my back. Turned out they were superficial. Lucky for me, the shrapnel hit between two grenades that I was carrying on the right side of my rucksack. Otherwise I would be dead. We were given credit for twenty kills." So, lucky or superficial means it can hurt like hell but you just don't die.

"The following morning, we walked into a huge bunker complex with plenty of blood trails, equipment and expended rounds-but no VC or weapons. In keeping with the VC's contact strategy, they took flight under cover of darkness to fight again another day. This contact was memorable because of its size as most contacts are "hit and run" lasting no more than five minutes. This is the type of contact that created major frustration on the part of my unit, which oftentimes led to roughing up the civilians in the area where the contact occurred. We just keep going back to the same area and take it over and over and over again"

I asked Sam what's with the number you kill. Why do you need to go count the people you just killed?

He said, "I believe it is because Nixon's Secretary of State, McNamara's background was in business, and it seemed to be his belief that the more we killed the quicker the enemy would surrender.

"It was at this time the Mobile Riverine Force was turned over to the South Vietnamese, and I was transferred to Delta Company, 6$^{th}$ division as a platoon leader. I had two fantastic staff sergeants who continually kept me on the right track. We continued to have several contacts which resulted in VC kills, primarily due to these two brave men. On the flip side, we suffered several booby trap wounds. By now I had gotten to know most of the officers and almost all of the men in my platoon. I really had a great group of men under me. They have a lot of guts and knew their jobs. Our last mission out was down to fifty-five men in the field. My platoon had only thirteen out of forty. This happens when men are pushed beyond their limits.

It is at this time that my feet are beginning to go bad even though I take ringworm pills, use ointment on my feet and change my socks every night in the field. First, I start with red spots all over my feet, then cracking and swelling and then knocked out of commission for about two weeks." Can you explain foot immersion a bit more? "If the skin became broken which happened frequently, you're in trouble and probably would remain on sick call for at least a week. I think beside trying not to get foot rot by walking around camp with flip flops to dry your feet out and perhaps a pill I think we were giving, not sure. Because of this we were given rarely a standard platoon size (forty-four men+ -) would result in around twenty or twenty-five men going to the field at one time. We were never at full strength due to foot problems.

I asked how often did the soldiers get down time.

With all we were going through these days we really needed what was called down time. But even then, it can get hectic. Especially when a lot of brass drop in for a visit. An example was when I got chewed out for letting the guys get a little drunk and swim in the river. My belief is my men deserve this break because my men do their job. They function well in the field under fire, they support each other, and they take orders. So, I have no real concern about what brass thinks. What can they do? Send me to Vietnam? It is such a mess here I sometime wonder if Washington even knows what they are doing.

A little later on, I contracted amoebic colitis, probably from drinking unclean water. I was hospitalized in Saigon and at the Cam Ranh Bay convalescent center. I went to Vietnam weighing 175 pounds. At the time of my hospitalization, I weighed 136 pounds.

Upon my return to the field, we were being employed in searches in the Plain of Reeds/Parrot's Beak area which was along the Cambodian border southwest of Saigon. This area was incredibly wet and my guys, including myself, suffered from continual foot problems. This region was a common entry point for North Vietnamese entering South Vietnam via the Ho Chi Minh Trail. Two tragedies occurred during this period. On a July night, we were set up on a night ambush along a river. There was a civilian curfew in this area that was continually violated by fishermen and other Vietnamese using the waterway during the nightly curfew periods. On this evening, even though they knew they had a curfew in this area, a sampan came down the river around 4 a.m. We fired on the sampan killing the male. One person drowned and we saved the others. It turned out to be a young father and his two children going to market. I've lived with this tragedy my entire life. Why couldn't he just wait till after curfew? The battalion commander flew into the local village and met with the village chief and the other. Compensation was made to the mother, but I never found out what it was or how much.

Two weeks later tragedy struck my platoon in the same area. Walking along a trail, we came to a gate and stopped to determine if there was a booby trap in the area. A command detonated mine went off. The explosion was enormous. Shrapnel rained down on everyone for some time. I was near the rear of our unit so I wasn't quite sure what happened. It was morning and we were returning to base camp after a night of ambushes. I'm sure it was a booby-trap as that was the VC's standard operating procedure around our base camp. I moved forward. The scene was sickening. Body parts were everywhere. It was hard to police up the parts and place them inside a poncho. Two were dead. One was severely wounded. The target was, Jerry White. Instead his radio operator and Kit Carson scout died from the detonated mine. Doing his job, Jerry had moved forward to check out a gate for bobby-trap wires. The tragedy took place shortly after the accidental deaths of the two Vietnamese civilians. Was that payback? I think so. For some forty-three years Jerry White has felt he should have died that day."

How do you find these "Kit Carson Scouts?"

"A Kit Carson scout is a Viet Cong who has rallied to South Vietnam side and worked as a paid mercenary for American troops. It is a name given to paid mercenary ($50.00/month). They were used to walk point (first in line) and communicate with individuals captured and /or villagers as we passed through various villages. My Kit Carson was about 18-22 years old and not particularly good at his job. These people were considered very expendable.

"I was taken out of the field and became an executive officer for the same company. This is a 'cushy' job with not much else to do but support the troops in the field by delivering food and ammunition when necessary. I also took my R&R leave and went to Taiwan, falling in love like every soldier does on his R&R. My unit was lucky enough to get to go to Cu Chi to see Bob Hope at Christmas time. We were airlifted to Cu Chi and sat in the hot sun to see Hope and his troops perform.

"On January 21st, 1970, Captain Everett Keaton, my company commander, was killed by a booby trap. As the executive officer, I was immediately ordered to take his place the following day. I was no more qualified to lead three different company platoons at this point in my military life. However, I did it and thanks to some great platoon leaders we managed to get through several operations without any casualties. There was one time, while out on a mission, that I should share only to show how humor can save you. We were in heavy contact with a sizable Viet Cong unit. We had maximum artillery and air support late in the afternoon. The smell, sights, and sounds are with me till this day. As darkness closed in, I yelled at a kid from Long Island "Pappy, shoot some ground flairs so we can see." (A ground flair is hand held, shot up in the air to provide lighting for improved vision.) A few moments later I heard members of my platoon start screaming and I saw sparks and flames ignited on the ground amongst us. I said .... Pappy, you dumb shit, what did you do? He said "I hit the ground flair like you said." I responded "Why the hell didn't you shoot up in the air." It said Ground Flair on the side of the tube." Now that is a very funny incident that was not funny at the time, but back at base we sure had fun giving Pappy the time of his life. To make fun of mistakes can relieve tension.

"I only had some forty-five days left in country and in the Army when this tragedy happened. In late March I received orders to rotate back to the United States. I left Bien Hoa Air Base on April 1st with memories of the two men killed and 13 wounded under my command as an infantry platoon leader. I still have thoughts and memories."

## Life After War

"The plane touched down at Travis AFB in California at four in the morning after a fueling stop in Tokyo. We were met in an assembly room by a staff sergeant who told us about the process of separation - medical evaluation, document signing and final payments. It would take about eight hours.

"I went to Vietnam alone. I came back from Vietnam alone. There was no 're-entry' plan for any of us. You signed a few papers, collected your money and returned home wherever that might have been. The memories were all yours to deal with as you saw fit. We were encouraged to sign a waiver regarding personal health as a way to speed up the separation process despite my various maladies. Despite a hearing loss from gunfire, artillery and gunships and the need for penicillin due to some over activity at the local Vietnamese massage parlor, I opted to separate as quickly as possible. The aforementioned governmental waiver was deemed illegal and was later eliminated as thousands of Vietnam veterans sought medical help from various VA hospitals.

"I flew home to Boston and was met by my mother. I was disappointed, but said nothing, that my father was not there after my entire year away from home. My brothers caught up with me eventually. I felt very uncomfortable back in the 'Real World.' I wondered if I fit in back here? There were no parties or excitement about my return.

"I decided to turn my thoughts to the future, but I really had no idea what I should pursue. I started with, due to weight loss, buying a new wardrobe. I also needed a job and it was at that time I was contacted by the CIA. They wanted me to go to Boston and be interviewed. I said no thank you."

Any idea why they called you?

"My belief was that certain things were done in Laos and Cambodia that were in secret and they needed combat ready soldiers to go in and train the Laotians.

"At that time the admissions department at my alma mater, Rollins College, contacted me to determine if I had an interest in becoming a counselor. I was comfortable with this idea as I had enjoyed my time at Rollins and it was something familiar to me. Better still, I could return to graduate school under the G.I. Bill and obtain a business degree. I knew I needed structure, direction and some purpose so, off to Rollins I went.

"While at home prior to going to Florida, I had a date arranged by a friend and his wife. While eating dinner, my date asked me what I had been doing recently and I explained that I recently separated from the Army after returning from Vietnam. She looked at me directly, with no understanding of what I just went through or what I am going through now, and said that if she had a brother who was eligible for the draft, she would have encouraged him to go to Canada. I felt as though I had been stabbed in the chest and the memory of this incident has stayed with me to this day. Talk about an epiphany! From this point on, I decided to keep my Vietnam experience to myself. All my feelings, thoughts and anger were put on the back burner and for the next 35 years. It was a longtime habit and I became very good at evading the subject by quickly changing the subject when military questions came up and simply pushed it to the back burner along with the anger that would re-appear every time the subject of Vietnam would come up.

"I completed graduate school with an MS in Business in the spring of 1973 and went to work for the Arnold Palmer Golf Company based in Chattanooga, Tennessee. Since I knew I had to work my entire life, I decided to associate myself within the golf industry. You might as well do something you love rather than not liking your avocation.

"Loneliness was pretty much my companion during these eight years - lots of drinking, a few casual relationships but no real place to share my loneliness, frustration, disconnection, or anger that I was feeling. My only salvation was playing golf.

"Along about this time I met my future wife and her eight-year-old son by a former marriage. Judy and Christian were Canadians based in

Montreal. This long-distance romance culminated in marriage in 1981 in New London, New Hampshire. For some reason it lacked passion."

I asked about lack of passion being due to long-distance.

He responded, "Maybe, or maybe little due to having deep feelings on the back burner for so long, just couldn't feel much. Looking back, there is no question that my work took precedence over family. Obviously, this lifestyle mirrored my father's family approach. Marriage became difficult with bouts of anger, detachment and insensitivity - the first inkling of future problems.

"It was in 1984 a welcome home event played out across the Nation. It was relatively mild and I'm not sure about the sincerity of the event. Part of me wanted to go to the event in Chicago but for some reason I decided not. It was at this time I began reading and in time became a fan of Nelson DeMille, a Vietnam veteran and a great writer of action novels. I have read pretty much all his works, two of which were about Vietnam. It was evident that DeMille had been an infantry platoon leader about the same as I had been in Vietnam. His writing was so real that I decided to send him a note about these two books. Close to two years went by and one day a letter arrived from DeMille and his publisher. It read:

*Dear Sam; Sorry for the delay in writing to you as I like to read and respond to all my own mail. Your comments were really nice and I appreciate the time you took to write to me.* ***Welcome Home Brother*** *Nelson DeMille*

"So, I finally got a home coming thirty-two years later.

"Around 1997, I felt issues concerning constant thoughts of Vietnam and potential business issues were leading to major depression. I thought of Vietnam daily, primarily those actions leading to wounding, death and wanton destruction of civilian villages. At the same time the Armour Company had been recently acquired. A new president was brought in and it appeared he wanted to clean house and install his own people. I saw my first psychologist. Although she was very good to me, I really did not believe she understood as to what I was going through. I stopped seeing her and just bottled thing up on the back burner again.

With all this going on in my head I became the third manager let go at Tommy Armour Golf Company. After 17 years of running the international division with 1998 estimated sales at twenty million, I was asked to sign a severance agreement. I said no and was given fifteen minutes to get out of the building. I hired a tough, Jewish lawyer who specialized in age discrimination. He took over the negotiation and turned a simple severance agreement into one three times larger. This result allowed me time to set up my own company with essentially a year's worth of funds.

I really wanted to do the entrepreneurial thing and decided to establish an export management company representing golf related, smaller companies that wanted to learn how to export their products. I loved the idea of working from home when I wanted. If I wanted to play golf on a Thursday, I could. If I wanted to work on Sunday morning, I could. There would be no bosses telling me what to do and when. I would be in my comfort zone. Working alone.

"Shortly after my first year, I was contacted by my good friend and Japanese golf equipment buyer, Hideki Satoh, to see if I was interested in joining forces and sharing profits under the name, Global Quest, Inc. We represented six to eight different companies from the USA, Canada, Indonesia, Sweden and the PRC. I believe it has been a wonderful association that continues today, even though we are both retired.

"With the advent of Facebook, it became easy to seek out old friends and acquaintances from the past. My relationship with Judy had evolved into 'two ships passing in the night' and I felt that there must be more to life than what had been happening the last several years. I made a decision to seek a divorce and move on with my life. The divorce took place in 2011 and I moved to Yarmouth Port, Ma.

"I decided to contact an old girlfriend from my days in Washington, DC. She joined me shortly thereafter. You can't go back in your life and capture what both had once known. We had changed. We stayed together as "roommates" - she upstairs, me downstairs for three years.

It was during this period that I descended into what I thought was just a deeper depression. I was quite unfamiliar with post-traumatic stress disorder at this point. I was not a very happy person and decided that it might be better to end my life. I obtained a license to carry gun license and even picked a spot at Bass River Golf Club as a place to end it all.

But, while doing work at the Nam Vets food pantry, someone suggested that I go over to the Hyannis Vet Center and check out their offerings. I spoke with the office manager there and then went home, thinking little about my visit.

A few days later I received a telephone call at nine one evening from Dr. Jocelyn Howard who introduced herself as the manager of the Hyannis Vet Center and asked me to drop by for a conversation. A call at nine p.m. - I was impressed. Someone actually cares about me. One visit turned into another visit and the next. Concepts such as survivor's quilt, anger issues, detachment, insensitivity, avoidance, surprises, crowds, security, unemotional attitudes, intimacy and self-esteem were touched upon. I realized that a lot of these concepts had hurt my marriage to the point of divorce.

I decided with Jocelyn's help to enroll in a four-month program taught by her. The program was called Cognitive Processing Therapy. This program requires lots of writing and weekly appointments with Dr. Howard. In summary, this program helps a veteran discuss and rearrange many of the issues in his daily life and memories of his time in Vietnam. The goal is to help the veteran rethink certain 'stuck points' in a more positive light. Individual sessions along with group therapy have been ongoing to this day. During this period, I received seventy percent disability from the VA. I take three different anti-depressants.

One thing I found through treatment was I had become emotionally numb with feelings of detachment and isolation from others. I have concentration problems with heightened sense of irritability and hyper-vigilance which impacted my daily functioning. What has happened to me was due to such experiences as witnessing one of my subordinate soldier's break-down and just killed civilians without authorization. Seeing a young father shot, a young daughter drowned, and one child saved." Eleven of his men were wounded and two were killed. "I was hardened by the war and was unable to feel pleasure or love. I was also wounded with shrapnel. This with many other happening during the war is why I have what is called PTSD. If I had not frozen myself on a back burner, I might have noticed a bit earlier. I give credit to a fantastic therapist that I am alive today. There are various treatment methods now underway, despite the fact that suicide rates in veterans continue to rise. Let's hope for more solutions.

"Judy and I remarried in 2016 and I have continued to work hard to improve my relationship as significant damage was done due to the divorce. Unfortunately, I was diagnosed with bladder cancer during this period and shortly I will undergo my fourth procedure for bladder cancer which will include a look at my kidneys. In 2017 I also developed an infected aorta directly related to the initial bladder cancer treatment. An eight-hour operation ensued. I am convinced that my bladder cancer was directly related to my exposure to Agent Orange chemicals in Vietnam. The VA has turned down my claim twice and a final decision will take place in Washington, DC with my lawyer and myself at a future date."

Sam's story is coming to an end. But while reviewing his interview he said, "For the past fifteen years I have expanded my knowledge of the Vietnam War. I have read over two hundred and fifty books on the subject. I was very naïve when I joined. My thoughts were very naïve. I had stayed that way since I buried my experience as a method of surviving. Experiencing the war and reading over the war has exposed me to the following thoughts....

1. Vietnam was a civil war.
2. Ho Chi Minh was the "George Washington" of Vietnam.
3. Kennedy, Johnson, McNamara and Westmoreland were responsible for 59,000 + deaths.
4. The war was limited by Washington DC Management.
5. Tried to fight a conventional war with well trained "hit +run" opponents who were committed to winning from day one.
6. I should have joined Vietnam Veterans against the War when I returned home.
7. Jane Fonda went way over the top with her anti-war activities
8. America seems to want to continue to be a policeman to the world.

**Questions on his experiences:**

1. Why do we have war?
   "We have war because the USA continually tries to be a 'Policemen to the World.' The sole thing I like about Trump is that he is extracting us from places like Syria, Iraq, Afghanistan and Yemen. Vietnam was the perfect example- a civil war where we got involved and should have let them find their own way."
2. What was the role of black soldiers?
   "I saw good black soldiers and bad ones, same as everyone. They stayed together and had little involvement with white, Native Americans or Hispanics."
3. What was the role of the media?
   "Occasionally we had newsmen imbedded with us – very infrequent. Commanders advised us not to discuss much with them."
4. How were women treated and what was their role?
   "I did not see enough American women to make a comment. My people were very polite to the Vietnamese that worked the base."
5. How were Gays and Lesbians treated?
   "Never discussed."

# CHAPTER 25

## *"One Hundred Percent" Bill Eugene Singleton - Heritage - English - Army*

I remember the first and only interview I had with Bill. I wished we could have continued that conversation. I miss his voice. It had a low somber tone that projected experience, pain, and wisdom. His eyes would be sharing the emotions of his words when you looked into them, and his physical state clearly showed the truth about war.

Before the second interview could happen, Bill died with help from the effects of Agent Orange and his time in a war zone. Bill's story will continue, with help from his wife who had saved his war letters, and from his brother Richard who shared their childhood days, before boot camp, war, and Vietnam.

In that first interview, I had asked how he ended up in Vietnam.

He said, "I was in Officer Candidate School in college and they told me if I stayed in OCS (Officer Candidate School) and graduated from college I would not be in the infantry or front-line type of things when and if I got drafted. Wrong. As soon as I graduated, I was drafted. I was assigned to the infantry. So much for promises."

He continued, "I graduated. I was drafted. I completed basic training at Ft. Lewis, Washington. I was awaiting shipment to the Military Intelligence School at Ft. Belvoir, Virginia. That is when all promises backfired. Somehow, I was caught up in a rushed formation for two new infantry battalions. It was an Infantry Regiment that would do training in the cold and snow without receiving any jungle training. Foolishly I thought I couldn't be destined for Vietnam. Wrong Again. So, Vietnam, here I come." It was getting late and Bill seemed to be tiring. We said we could meet again and he gave me a file of all his letters home, that his wife had filed in order of dates, so I might go through them.

**Before Vietnam** - As remembered by Bill's brother Richard

It begins with two brothers living in a small house adjacent an apple orchard. Richard explains, "As far as our first eight years of living we shared a house which allowed one room for a small kitchen. That space was also called the living space. A small addition was bedroom space for all five of us. We did not have a bathroom in house but we had a two-seater out back. For us kids a two-seater wasn't so bad." It was an adventure every time we entered. You never knew what you would find. The two-seater and the apple orchard lasted eight years. Then off to a wheat farm we went."

Next question was what did eight- and nine-year-old boys do with their spare time. Bill loved this period of time the most of any of our childhood time. We had to do things like milk the cows, feed the chickens, and then collect eggs every morning for breakfast. I hated that part of the day, but Bill would say 'as long as we're outside, being alone and doing what we want, just be happy.'

He was right. After work we could roam free around the whole ranch and farm as long as we got back by meals. I agree with Bill when he would say 'Summers are the best'. Best because we got to, at the age of eight and nine to in the combine some and in the truck that would take the wheat from the combine while both vehicles kept moving.

We played a lot of cowboys and Indians back then and a lot of army. We had a creek that ran through the ranch, and when it was dry it was a great place to play hide and seek. During the snow melt and run off it would get high and move fast and we played Army. It was always Bill who got to pick the game. He was the oldest. When I asked why he always picked army he replied 'because I might have to do this someday.' Little did we know then."

When I asked about his parents and what type of work they did, Richard said, "Bill and I knew our dad was a disciplinarian, and we would get whipped pretty often with belts, switches or whatever was handy. But we understood he was just doing what he had gone through with his father and brothers. We also understood he was a good man, husband, and father. He was definitely a hard worker. He became the main maintenance man and machinery fixer on the wheat farm.

Our mom," he said, "was just as hard a worker as my dad. When we moved to the wheat farm, she had her work cut out for her. While my dad was the maintenance man for the machinery, my mom was the cook for over twenty guys including us five. It is hard for some to imagine that in the fifties there still were traveling bunkhouses and cookhouses. But there were, and my mom was in charge. Cooking for over fifteen hungry people, three times a day. The bunkhouse and cookhouses traveled with us because time was money. Work was from sun up to sun down just like the cattle men of the old west, with never a day off.

After eight years of such a life, our mom had enough. She said to our dad that we are moving to the city about thirty miles away and get a 'real life.' She said he could come if he wants. She began packing. He came. After moving to the new city, Wenatchee Washington, which had about thirty-five thousand people, things began to change. Neither Bill nor I wanted to change. We had our fun, friends and freedom and now we are losing it. Bill never liked the new school. He was the new kid, and he was small framed and only five-five. He never had a girlfriend in school and now that I look back, he was a little anti-social. For jobs, we had to help our dad at his night job which was that of janitor. If we wanted any money, we would work in the fruit season picking cherries or apples.

As with all kids we grow up and move apart. Bill went off to college. The distance was over an hour from home so I really didn't get to see him much after that. During college he worked summers with the Forest Service on the Trail or Brush crew. He loved being outdoors and hiking the woods. I remember that he liked being alone a lot."

**<u>Time in Vietnam</u>** - Recalled through letters home.

Bill's letters explained the trip over to Vietnam.

"It was a very sobering sight and the atmosphere among us suddenly became considerably more restrained, even before we left ground. We were being held on the plane while several buses and ambulances loaded casualties from the war onto a transport plane. We saw many more trailers come loaded with silver military caskets. I do believe at that moment every one of us had our own misgivings about what lay ahead for us." Bill had not left the states yet when he saw the casualties of war returning home. He hadn't even landed in Vietnam yet and he was already feeling the war. He continued, "We then head out. We fly over the Bataan Peninsula where we were reminded of the WWII battle. Over 4,500-men were either killed or moved into captivity as part of the infamous Bataan Death March. I really did not need a history reminder at this time.

Finally landed in Vietnam, we arrived at Bien Hoa, twenty miles northeast of Saigon. We were then moved, by truck, to Camp Bearcat. Armed guards were on each vehicle. Several jeeps with mounted machine guns were positioned in front and rear of the convoy. On our way we passed through several small hamlets, clusters of hooches, (grass houses). They were for the most part small, filthy shacks with pigs and chickens running loose...and the smell! The people looked dirty and wore pajamas, thongs (sandals), and conical straw hats. The kids ran alongside begging for food or cigarettes. As we traveled, we heard shots ring out. We all went to the floor except the guard. He just grinned at us and said 'Relax. They are only hunting rats for food.' So, this was my welcome to a very new environment.

It is really sad watching the Vietnamese collecting garbage, going through it and taking out good food. We must have given away a box of oranges and apples to the many women who go from mess hall to mess hall. We are told that the people will help us do odd jobs for food or money. Many of the young girls prostitute themselves (much to the loud encouragement of the troops) The workers earn $.80 a day and GI's will pay five dollars for 'short time' (quick sex) I can only imagine what the people think of us."

Bill talked about his first trip out and he wrote, "I know now why the war is lasting so long. The reason the war is lasting so long and we can't catch the VC (Viet Cong), who carry only a rifle, ammo and some rice while a small framed guy like my 130 lbs. needs to carry: canteens of water, purification tablets, 'boonie hat,' mosquito repellent, first aid pack, eight rifle magazines, two fragmentation grenades, twenty- one boxes of ammo, eighteen M-79 rounds - nine extra pounds, for me, one M-16 rifle (and an M79 grenade launcher for me), bayonet, cleaning kit, field rations, helmet, and flak jacket and that's just the half of it. I believed what I carried really outweighed me."

He came back to my question of first trip out, and he replied, "We're ready to go out on our first real, deep jungle recon in force patrol tomorrow, away from the safety of the base. We are apprehensive, but I think we will do okay. We are rested, and at full strength. About thirty minutes into the jungle I changed my mind, I believed we are now in hell, even before we meet the enemy," he repeats saying, "We're so in Hell! The triple canopy jungle is frightening, with its thick undergrowth of vines, thorns, marshy areas, red ants, that burn when they bite, snakes that kill when they bite, damn mosquitoes that never stop, streams all filled with leaches and other bugs like large scorpions. The foliage is so thick that very little sunlight gets to the ground. It seems like we were lost most of the time. We could hardly hear our copters, much less see them - or them us. So much for our air support! The only consolation is according to our CO (commanding officer) was that the jungle up north, where we were originally going, was much worse." The thought of a year here is so very depressing. Any 'romantic' view of war I might have had, has definitely been shaken."

He continued, saying, "Some more about contact my squad had recently engaged in. We went out to set up an ambush where the last unit was hit. It was quite a distance and we weren't very happy about being that far out by ourselves and this soon after the fighting, as the VC sometimes comes back to the area to retrieve hidden weapons and maybe their dead.

"So, we are boating upstream to set our ambush and we pass a bombed pagoda. We took a vote and decided to set up. We told the boat operator to pick us up in the morning. We reasoned no one would be the wiser and we would be safer. We called in our position as to where we should be and settled in for the night. Unfortunately, we were not so safe, we had set up along the trail to a nearby VC hamlet. It began to rain. It was damp and dark and miserable and that was when we heard the cry from the guy posted about ten meters from us. He opened up with his M-60 machinegun and we saw several people running toward our direction. I opened fire and two went down. I heard a commotion to the rear and turned to see a dink trying to crawl away with a bullet wound in his chest."

What were your thoughts on this type of fighting?

Bill said, "It is really like Russian roulette. It is like we insert a platoon or company size unit into a pre-selected site to sweep the area in hopes of making contact with the enemy. If contact is made, the other units, like us, on standby are flown in to 'circle and engage the enemy with superior firepower.' What usually happens is the inserted unit gets mauled before help arrives. So, if we find nothing then we are picked up and inserted into another area. Sooner or later our luck will run out and there you have Russian roulette. What I learned is no John Wayne stuff here. It will get you wasted and for what. We just leave and the VC just comes back.

We moved forward again, we hit more bunkers and booby traps and took some casualties. My buddy was killed right in front of me and the thought that it could have been me was so frightening as to be beyond description. I blame myself for him getting killed – I was walking point and got mired down in the mud so he went around me and he was the one that got shot.

That night shells were falling so close that some of the shrapnel was landing amongst us. I was wounded the morning of the second day by a grenade explosion as we started to push into the nipa (a species of palm) toward the bunkers. Two fellow soldiers helped carry me back to the landing zone.

Sometime later after dozing off I was awakened by a burst of fire. A dink between me and a hooch had fired at noises, which come daylight we discovered the noise was a pig. I feel bad for the pig because I think it was the moaning all night. Believe me that was the worst night of my life and I have never been so scared. Next day I was medevaced (medical evacuation) back to Dong Tam in a small LOACH copter (OH-6 Cayuse, a light observation helicopter nicknamed LOACH).

"I'm to have surgery to remove shrapnel and have stitches in my legs, butt and under my armpit. At the end of the day I had stitches in five wounds, and we pretend and say 'We were so Lucky.' I think lucky would (be) not to be here at all. What I want most is to just lie down in the shade of a pine tree, next to a bubbling creek, and look out on a mountain lake and drink clean, cold, pure sweet water till I burst. You wouldn't believe what some of the guys do to stay here (at the hospital). They pull scabs off, spray their wounds with lighter fluid, and even put dirty bandages back on. It is wrong, but if the conditions are as bad up north as they say, and all of them say the same, I can't really blame them. The doctor came in this morning and said I would be discharged day after tomorrow. I'm to go straight to my unit, not Class 1 condition wing for a bit more recuperation. I'm going to be hurting if I have to start humping the paddies after lying around for a month. I'll try to get light duty profile before I leave because of the continued drainage from the one wound.

So, I arrive at Dong Tam yesterday after being detailed as a guard with a supply convoy going south from Bearcat. My medical release will keep me out of the field for a few days more but it won't keep me out of work detail. Guess due to no physical work, I will be answering phones and typing reports. According to our Intel, a VC offensive is supposed to start soon and LBJ has stopped the bombing. It is a political move and has every one over here mad as hell as it frees Charlie to move about easier and prepare to attack us. The next morning, we were placed on alert after Delta Company ran into trouble out in the Plain of Reeds, an area of rice paddies and large nipa groves that extends into Cambodia. Perez said that until new orders came down, I was going in with the company. Perez was such a SOB. I really tried to stop hating him but it used too much energy so I just stopped.

I have seen a few of another type over here beside the ones who pull scabs off. These guys actually enjoy the fighting and killing. Some of them have been here for several tours and keep volunteering to come back. I believe this war has done something to these guys. They are like animals. I'll have to admit there is a certain exhilaration to some of the things we do, but the fear exhaustion and loss of buddies heavily outweighs it. I have heard of incidents where prisoners have been shot. I suspect that this is from a combination of frustration at not being able to fight the enemy face to face and losing friends to mines and booby traps, which we suspect are often set by the civilians in the area, who are also selling us things. We all have less compassion for the people, guilty or innocent. I wonder just how much I have changed?

We ended up about a mile out of Saigon on Highway 15 with nothing but rice paddies around us. Did it ever rain. I was huddled under my poncho, which leaked, trying to get some sleep. I really thought I was dreaming when the cutest little girl, about five, dropped in during the cloudburst. She just popped in, with the sweetest little shy grin on her face. She looked at me and just crawled under my poncho. After the rain stopped, she just crawled out, smiled at me and was on her way. When the rain finally stopped, we just began to freeze the rest of the night. I really wish I could take pictures of all of these so later years we could look back when feeling blue and be thankful for what we have. Little kids back home dream of toys, over here they dream of food and safety.

We are back to heavy fighting at a river crossing. My platoon never came under fire and my only involvement was to take all spare ammo magazines we had up to the guys fighting. Although I was not directly in the mi(d)st of the fighting, I did have a very close call. While moving out through a rice paddy I was suddenly knocked back onto my ass into about two feet of water. I did not know what happened until I picked up my helmet and found that I was hit by a bullet. It went through the steel pot, through the fiberglass liner and lodged into my wallet. Thank God. I never even heard the shot fired

This prolonged time in the field without rest and a chance to dry out is starting to tell on our feet. Almost each day there is someone taken out, usually because of feet immersion. There are many guys just waiting to get back to see the doctor. Mine are starting to really crack and get big sores. It probably will take another week of field duty before I'd qualify for a profile. There have been cases of guys constantly keeping their feet wet and their boots on to speed up the problem. The mud is a dirty coal black and it smells bad – really bad. I recall my uncle told me of the Koreans dumping human waste on fields for fertilizer.

They are trying to cut down the numbers of guys on profile and thus out of the field, therefore we are no longer permitted to go to the medical facilities at the camp. There they don't usually see ailments like ours that are common to infantry troops in the Delta. They will give us a week's profile for feet in not too bad condition. Here at the battalion aid station, the condition has to be really bad to get a profile. Back to work. We are now guarding a radar site about four miles south of camp. Actually, we may be guarding the radar gear from the ARVN's (Army of the Republic of Viet Nam, the South Vietnamese army). It seems to me that we worry more about them than the VC. We are in a half-finished hut. It is open at both ends. I swear my eyes are playing tricks on me. I just saw a chicken. It walked right across the room in front of me. Nope, there it goes again. Two of them this time. Shit, here comes a pig. It is a little pig. This is it; I'm calling a halt to anything bigger. I just closed my eyes.

About midnight our company was inserted, a risky operation even with a full moon, into an area where a rocket site was reported. Things started to go wrong right from the start. Our platoon was put down in the wrong area. When we did manage to link up with the rest of the company, we were separated by the river. Then our radio went on the blink and we lost contact with everyone. Next morning everyone was flown out, except us. The helicopter that was sent for us wouldn't land at our site as the pilot didn't think it was secure enough. So, we had to hump four miles away to get to a truck that could bring us to safety.

Got hit again. I got wounded in both knees and (my) side. My rifle and pack had been destroyed by shrapnel, probably saved my life. So, I am unarmed, cannot move, and the damn mosquitoes were having a Thanksgiving dinner on me. That was the longest and worst night of my life. I had never in my life been so scared. The next day I was medevaced in a small LOACH copter. Thank God for the medic and several others who crawled over and bandaged me up and helped me back up about a mile from the action. Those guys just don't get enough credit. They just don't.

I need to go for more x-rays because of the stomach wound isn't healing. There are fragments still lodged up against my stomach and haven't moved. I really think I should have gone to the hospital instead of pulling work details where I don't get any rest. Right now, I am so restless, so wound up, and so nervous. Maybe someday I won't jump when an artillery round is fired. The bunker I am assigned to is on the corner of the base. Right now, they are spraying defoliation chemicals on the high grass and nipa palm to our front. It really is beautiful to watch, which I found out later it was Agent Orange. Didn't know the affects it would have on my entire life and my bad health.

Some days, like today, while sitting in my bunker and I see the sun rise, it is like a huge orange ball with palm trees and hooches silhouetted against the horizon….so very beautiful. Then the fog comes in and hides it all. When the fog lifts, I can see a little girl is trying to drive a bunch of chickens into a pen. An old woman (is) squatting down behind the wall of a crude toilet. Another woman is trying to take a pig to market. The pig has a rope tied to its head and front leg. Hope this little pig gets to market, on three legs. For some reason I am just laughing. Maybe because I am going crazy or just the story of 'The Three Little Pigs' come to mind. Anyway, some little kids are going off to school. The girls are wearing white pants, shirts and straw hats. The boys have blue shorts and white shirts and caps. The older girls are wearing ankle length gowns, with either black or white pants. These girls were very, very attractive. Just to add a bit more, we watched a young woman take a bath in the pond. Thanks to our starlight scope. The clarity of the view was great! This to me was a family just like ours who just want to live, work, and play. I really feel bad for them. They are in the middle of all the players in this war.

Here is a good story for you. It is not always the enemy you must watch out for. As we were being mortared last night, I ran back to my bunker. I ran by the dog compound. I went by a large dog who lunged at me with only his chain to stop him. As I jumped backward to get away, he bit right on the tip of my penis, drawing blood. I immediately went weak in my knees and had visions of life without sex or kids. At the aid station the doctor cleaned the little tear off with disinfectant and said that I was lucky because the dog had just had his rabies shots. The Commanding Officer reportedly got a good laugh when he heard of the incident. I probably won't even have a scar to show off and no Purple Heart. Everyone but me thought it was hilarious.

"We are getting busy for the IG (Inspector General) Inspection. Talk about stupidity: boots, hats and belts must be marked with name, rank, and serial number. The VC threats are taken (sic) second place to this affair. I wonder how the line units in the field handle this kind of info? I cannot believe this can happen to those guys in the field. Guess I have just come to know that anything is possible in Vietnam. We were just told that when this is over, we will be getting more defoliation chemicals for the nipa in front of us.

We are now in March and I am heading home in fifteen days and I am done with Vietnam. Thank God, Thank God, Thank God. I am so upbeat and happy. I just thought of a funny to share. Did I ever tell you about the cussing lizards? It is about one foot long and has a cry that sounds like F**k You! F**k You! They repeat those sounds several times and then become silent for a time. Just thought that story would help me stop thinking about only fifteen more days to go, otherwise if I keep thinking about it, I will be jinxed. I am now going to sleep until I wake, even if it goes through noon chow. I am almost there. I wonder how much I have changed? They are going to defoliant (sic) the grass in front of the riverside bunkers this afternoon. Guess I have already started to leave. I've taken to spending much of my free time in the safety of my bunker. I do not go outside after dark and I just count the days, less than one week to go and good bye Vietnam.

"Today is the day. I am on Pan Am flight to Oakland, California. I can't express the relief I felt as I watched the coastline move out of sight. The cheers that went up when we took off was something to behold, otherwise the mood was mostly subdued."

**After Vietnam** as remembered by his brother Richard

"As far as family and home, I remember going out to dinner with the family and he was very nervous. He sat with his back to the wall. When the waiter dropped something or someone would make a loud noise he would jump from the unexpected. He seldom talked about his experience over there other than in generalities and generic things about the weather or the geography or something about the people but not about the day to day involvements or conflicts. As he got older, he did tell me a few things like he was wounded twice. The first was the worse. But, between the two he was left with injuries to both legs, knees, back, buttocks and under his arm. Some of these injuries never really healed and gave him trouble his whole life. Several pieces of shrapnel were left and not removed for some reason.

As he got older, he developed more and more health problems. I can't remember them all. I know he had issues with the old wounds. His feet from the leaches and bad water that his feet were always in. I think it was called foot rot. He had prostate problems, type 2 diabetes, blood pressure problems, and the last few years of his life were with an oxygen tank due to severe breathing problems. An MRI was done and the result showed a growth in his lungs that appeared to be a fungus."

He stayed up nights with these conditions. He couldn't get any relief and had a difficult time laying down. He believes strongly that these disabilities were all due to Agent Orange and other chemicals used in Vietnam. He believes this due to the many times he was exposed to it.

Toward the end of Bill's life, the government put him up to forty per cent for disabilities. I saw Bill and during our interview it was my impression that disability should have been rated much higher. I say that not as a journalist but as an Occupational Therapist. He was totally one-hundred per cent disabled.

As I said, Bill died, with only 40% of our government's support.

# CHAPTER 26

*"Humor til the End" Bill Arcuri - Heritage Italian - Airforce*

## Life Before the War

Bill's wonderful sense of humor is probably what helped him through his stint as a POW during the Vietnam War. I experienced that sense of humor when I had the good fortune of sitting at his kitchen table listening to the bantering of six or seven veterans. They are from different wars, different branches and different ages. None of that mattered. You could see that they were as close as brothers could be. I somehow felt that I was intruding in a private club and yet I never thought to leave. If the world could have each other's back like these guys we probably would not need wars.

I start our conversation by asking Bill about his family and with no hesitation he responded. "Michael is my dad's name and he was first generation Italian, one of five siblings. He joined the Army after high school to get out of the old coal mining town of Frackville, Penn. He met my mother while stationed at the old Army Air Corps base in Tallahassee, Fla. He was very strict with the older kids growing up which I think was pretty normal back then. Big difference on how us first three were raised from the three younger ones. He was very career orientated and spent a lot of time going to night school to get his college degree. He was, in my mind, a really hard-working man"

His next comment was about his mom. "My mother Lila, on the other hand, was the youngest of ten siblings raised in Tallahassee, in a home with dirt floors. As a child she hunted and fished and really enjoyed the outdoors. I remember one time where she took me fishing and swimming in the Banana River. We caught the fish, cleaned them and just sat right down and cooked them over a fire. That was one of my best childhood memories. She held the family together during the times my dad was gone, like when he was in England during WWII, and then another time when he was deployed to Alaska. She was a great cook and a great seamstress, a great mom who I think was the glue that kept our family together. By the way, she was also a Blue Star Mother with the three oldest children serving during the Vietnam War."

We stopped in order to let the others at the table have time to tell a bit about their childhood. When things settled down and coffee was poured Bill began telling about his childhood. He said "there were six siblings, Michael, Patty, Me, Sherry, Steve and Philip. As far as growing-up, I pretty much did what I was told. I was the middle child so my older brother and sister and the two younger brothers got most of the attention. I was a cutup in school, bringing home A's and "Needs Improvement" in conduct. From age fourteen until eighteen I was in the Boy Scouts. Got my Eagle award and was Junior Assistant Scout Master for my Boy Scout Troop at Patrick AFB. I really enjoyed camping and outdoor activity.

The two years we were in Alaska were totally surrounded by nothing but untouched nature. For us kids it was unbelievable. When you left the base it really was like you still see in books like National Geographic." His face changes like he was going back in time and a little smirk appeared on his lips. He continues with, "one dumb thing I remember as a kid was, while living in Alaska, I rode my bike down a highway that was just resurfaced and I totally messed up my bike with oil. Because of that dad decided I needed a little more discipline so off to military school and that is how I ended up at West Point years later." He takes a moment to get back to the present and says, "Then back to Bedford, Mass. We lived off base in the small town and our back yard was close to the Concord River and nature preserve. We played in the woods, in the overflow. We grew a large garden during spring and summer. Never spent much time inside except for winter. When we moved to Patrick AFB, Florida we lived on the barrier reef. While waiting for our base housing we lived on Silver Beach which was right on the ocean. He said, "We literally walked out the back door and over the sand dunes to the beach. When we finally moved into the base house it was just a quarter mile from the ocean and right on the Banana River. As a kid I remember helping my dad and neighbor build a dock in our back yard so we could tie up the boats. It was a great childhood fishing, swimming, sailing right in your own back yard. If we weren't in the river, we were over by the Officer's Club on the ocean.

As far as games, we played the normal games growing up, Hide and Seek, Red Rover, Mother May I, freeze tag. Also played badminton, croquet. As older kids freeze tag became bicycle tag. We also, would sneak out and go over to the Concord River overflow and would go sliding/skating on the ice. Something, not allowed today, was we would play on the railroad tracks and place pennies on the track when a train would come by and collect our flattened pennies. The best ever was when we lived at Patrick AFB, Fla. my older brother and I with other friends would sneak into the B-17s that were parked on the maintenance ramp by the boathouse and play 12 o'clock high. That was a highlight of my life.

"I really was a runt growing up, small for my age, but that didn't stop me from playing to win. I was on the wrestling team at the AF Academy Prep School and while at West Point, I was on the gymnastic team and I could clear 9.5 ft. pole vaulting unless it was an aluminum pole then it was a clear 10 feet."

When did you decide the military was for you? He said, "I think it was around sixth grade that I started to think about what I wanted. I had been around the service culture since I could remember and after we arrived at Patrick AFB, Florida, living on an airbase with the river as our back yard and the ocean as our front yard it was really exciting for me. Being on base during the airshows and especially with the missile program. All the original astronauts were flying in and out and it wasn't uncommon to see them on base. After each launch they would be brought back to Patrick AFB. Most of my neighbors were pilots. We lived through the Cuban Missile Crisis while at Patrick AFB and I think all of this had a great impact on my wanting to become a pilot and serve in the Military. Most all of my dad's and mother's brothers had served during WWII and that also had an impact on me. As a matter of fact, I think the Air Force was my first full time job. Before that I babysat, mowed grass or had a paper route." Seems like you were born to fly and his reply was "I grew up in a military family on a military base my whole life. I was born Italian, raised Catholic, but I think the Air Force got in my blood. So, I joined."

Is that what makes a patriot? Just asking.

## Life During the War

My first question was, 'When did you join'? His response, "On graduation from high school I enlisted in the Air Force and attended the Air Force Academy Preparatory School but only received a qualified alternate appointment to the Air Force Academy, but I also received a Congressional Appointment to West Point. So, I took the sure thing and attended West Point from 1966 to 1970. There were many flying opportunities in the Army but that changed in 1968 when the decision was made that the main flying in the Army would just be helicopters. That is when I made the decision to take a commission in the Air Force upon graduation which was still available at that time."

So, you are there and what was your first Impression of Vietnam, the environment and people. He replied, "I have to say that since I was flying the B-52 aircraft I was never really in Vietnam proper. We were stationed at Guam AFB and Utapao AFB, Thailand. The large percentage of my missions were flying out of Guam." I asked if he could start with his first encounter to when he was shot down. "Since I never actually was in Vietnam my life flying combat from Guam was pretty much like living on a normal air force base in the states except it was a 24 hour operation every day. We had three days of flight then another three days as Duty Crew, which entailed prepping B-52s, then to be used as backups if one of the scheduled B-52s had to abort it's takeoff. After all that we would get three days off which we used to just relax and spend the day on the beaches of Guam.

Can you speak about your time as a Prisoner of War in Hanoi

Hilton? Bill began with, "We were into our second sixth-month rotation when there was a stand-down from flying. I wondered if it was a good sign. But no, all our positive thoughts of going home just dissipated. We were called into a meeting; we were all tense with fingers crossed that this meeting was to say we are going home. Nope, instead we are told 'Gentlemen we are going to North Vietnam.' That is when we found out that the North Vietnamese Delegation had walked away from the Peace Talks in Paris. Back to bombing. No going home yet. So, I ask Bill what's next? Bill said, "Back to war with President Nixon ordering a full-scale bombing of North Vietnam. This campaign would become known as Line Backer II which would be a three-day bombing campaign in the month of December 1972. Our crew was scheduled for day three so we preformed Taxi Crew, Duty Crew for the initial two days. On the first night of Line Backer II, there were 129 B52s scheduled in three waves. Five B52s were hit and three were lost, two over North Vietnam. On night two there were ninety-three B52s scheduled in three waves. Two B52s were hit by surface to air missiles and one crashed landed in northern Thailand. There were ninety-nine B52s scheduled in three waves. Seven B52s were hit by surface to air missiles, four over North Vietnam, one lost over Laos, one lost over Thailand and one landed in Thailand.

Day three, and it was my 44^th^ mission and I remembered the night before we had just been talking about going to the same altitude, the same type of targets and the same route every night. We wondered who thought the enemy was not going to catch on. We knew that they were not dumb. It was my 44^th^ mission and we were shot down over North Vietnam during the first wave. We knew it, we sensed it, because we knew the enemy was not dumb.

We got hit, we maintained control but then we began descending 3,000 ft. Just as I began to speak, the pilot said 'Crew looks like this is it'. I turned to look and he had ejected. The crew followed him. My turn. We are trained for this, but never really prepared for reality.

We understood the physical and mental part but the unknown is always a stressor. So, I am going down and with my luck, I had to land in a bamboo field. I have bamboo sticking up the inside of my helmet and bamboo stuck in my arm. I was in lots of pain but that physical training kicks in, and I see this little old lady coming toward me, I take the bullets out of my gun and threw them, take the batteries out of my radio and crush them and since I had bamboo between the inside of my helmet and my head I threw my helmet to the side. She is closer and I am thinking thank God it is a little old lady. God didn't have time to get my message because that little old nasty lady wacked me so hard on the side of my head with her hoe, then a tall angry looking fellow comes up and grabs my gun, points it at my head and began 'shooting' at me. So, I think 50-50 is not bad. I did take the bullets out before he could kill me but should have left my helmet on." I asked how can you joke at such a time? "Easy, it is what keeps us sane."

I should not have interrupted Bill so, I asked if he would continue. He said, "After the nasty little grandmother and her large tall relative were done, I was besieged by local villagers, beaten and stripped of all my equipment and flight suit. It was then that four local Militia pulled me away from the villagers and protected me until I was transferred As I began checking my aches and pains, I found I had received injuries to my arms and legs due to flailing from the ejection. As a result, I dislocated my right knee on impact with the ground. I had a bamboo shoot in my arm and a rather large bash on my head.

With all this going on, four militia come up to me, each took an end of me and one put his foot on my crotch and pulled my leg. Later I found out that what he did saved my life.

Then I was moved into a hooch for safety and there was this old Vietnamese man and he just turns to me and asked if I would like a cig. I said I don't smoke. But then I looked at him and he seemed, crazy as it sounds, disappointed. So, I take his cig and smoked it. Didn't choke. I take another look at him and I realize that this old and tired man was just trying to live. He must get up at dawn and begin plowing his fields, gather rice, and just wanting a piece of land to farm and a house for his family. I smile and then greet the militia that is coming in. They tie my hands and blindfold me. One of the militia guys saw that the rope was on my wound and he came over and moved it. It sounds crazy but it happened.

They had all prisoners put on a bus and that is where I heard my co-pilot's voice. Terry, you ok? And the answer was 'yes'. I can't tell you what a feeling of knowing no matter where you are ending up you are not alone. We could not talk any longer because this guy with a machete walks up and down the aisle. I knew if I laughed, he would probably cut off my head. But, even with that in mind he reminded me of Charlie Chan (old time movie detective) and I had to keep repeating in my head don't laugh, don't laugh. We were then put in the hospital and I was given a very hot needle that was just shoved in 'Holy Cow' was all I could say, it hurt'. Next day I got a bamboo splint on my leg and then thrown into a cell where I landed on something soft. It was our gunner Roy. Again, feelings of not being alone. We are now on a boat, and all I can think of is a hot shot American pilot looking down and saying 'Hey, look! a boat.' I spent one night in the field and then transported to the Hanoi Hilton the next day. I am in prison. I'm thrown into a cell through a big steel door. My blindfold is taken off and it is pitch black. Then I have a blanket and net thrown into my cell and then I hear a key turn. I get a little up tight. I take a moment to check that I am in about a 6 ft by 6 ft cell room with a wood floor and a little table and chair. My first five days in captivity I was in solitary confinement with little food and daily interrogated. Every morning, I was taken to a room and there if I answered, what they thought was wrong, they would bend my broken leg. I was moved into a larger cell with eight other wounded airmen on Christmas Day. From the 20$^{th}$ until the 28$^{th}$ of December it was quite an experience with all the daily and nightly bombings. From the 28$^{th}$, until January 28$^{th}$ it was pretty calm since the bombings had stopped and the days became routine as the older prisoners said not to worry as they felt it was over. I was pretty much on my back most of the time during this period as I was unable to walk with my leg injuries. On January 29$^{th}$ it was announced that the Peace Agreement had been signed and that we may be going home. We were all beside ourselves, especially the eight-year guys.

At that time, I was moved into another section of the prison with all the sick and wounded. It became apparent that the sick and wounded POWs would be released first but did not know when that day would come. For some guys it was hard knowing but not knowing when we would go. For me this time was really relaxed and I spent my time discussing what had happened during the time the older POWs were held and answering any questions that they might have. Still only received limited food and no medical care to speak of. On the morning of February 12th, the guards came in and gave us a change of clothes and transported us to the Gia Lam Airport. I was released with the sick and wounded and flew out of North Vietnam and arrived at Clark AFB in the Philippines. As hard as I had it, I have to say that the only similarity between my POW experience compared to the older POWs was my last mission and initial week in captivity. After that there is no comparison."

## Life After the War

"Operation Homing" was the plan to bring the American POWs home. It started on February 12th and lasted until March 29th, 1973. The POWs returned in groups which coincided with the pullout of American Troops from South Vietnam. The first step was to get the POWs to Clark AFB and to medical treatment and evaluation. I was on the first flight into Clark AFB. Since my internment has only been fifty-five days I was evaluated and put on the first flight back to the United States on February 15th. With a refueling stop at Hickam AFB, Hawaii and then to Travis AFB, California where we landed on February 14th. Travis AFB was the initial Medical Facility for all the northern California bases. Since I was stationed at Beale AFB in Yuba City California this was home for me. On arrival I was reunited with my wife and later that day my folks arrived from Florida. After being discharged from Travis AFB I returned home to Yuba City and received six months of physical therapy. I came back from Vietnam different. My wife could tell something was wrong but couldn't understand it. I don't think I understood it either. It took me thirty-three years before I finally received treatment at the local VA for PTSD. It was then that I heard her say "I have my husband". That was thirty-three years after my return from war.

After I separated from my first real job, six years in the Air Force, I worked for the Electronic Data Systems whose HQ was in Dallas,

Texas. The company was owned by H. Ross Perot. I worked there for twelve years until it became General Motors. But, a year later, I joined Perot Systems INC again and worked there for the next 24 years until I retired."

## Questions

1. Why do we have wars?
   That is a good question. It would be nice if there were no wars but as long as there is evil in the world, we need to be in a position to protect ourselves and if that means fighting a war, so be it.
2. What was the role of the media?
   The role of the media should just be reporting the news.
3. What was women's role in the war?
   During Vietnam the role of women was administration and medical (nurses, doctors).
   Today that has changed to include combat positions.
4. How were gay and lesbian soldiers treated in the war?
   As far as I know they were not treated any differently than other soldiers. We need to stop putting labels on individuals.
5. What was treatment for PTSD?
   The main treatment today, for PTSD is medicine, and counseling. Not sure there was much treatment for anything when we first got home.
6. What was the role of black soldiers?
   Knowing the history of the Black Soldiers through WWII, I believe there is no difference today. We don't have Black Soldiers, only American Soldiers.
7. What would you tell young people today about joining the service?
   Project 425 does career days at many local schools. We talk about the many job opportunities there are in the service and the benefits of serving and then using the GI Bill to continue with your education.

8. Would you do it again?
   Having a strong relationship with the South Vietnamese in our local area, and the respect they have for America, and the Vietnam Veterans who fought for their country, Yes, I would do it again.

# CHAPTER 27

*"Doc" Roger Landry - Air Force Flight Surgeon*

## Life Before the War

Roger is a childhood friend of my husband Charlie, and that is how I met this gentleman. He wore a wide brimmed hat, and salt/pepper gray beard and a genuine smile. His words were spoken in a soft, slow manner which made me feel he was comfortable and had no need to rush off. Again, over coffee, I ask my first question:

Can you just tell a bit about your childhood? He said, "I believe because my mom was taken out of school and put to work around the age of twelve, she was going to make sure that my brother and I, would have the opportunity for a good education. My father would work many hard hours and my mother was a very frugal homemaker to make sure that we would have that opportunity. They did not do the work alone. They made sure that we knew what hard work was. They made sure that we were prepared to be independent in the world. Some of the things that they did might seem harsh in today's world but they always had our best interest at heart. We were boys soon to be men and we were going to be responsible, tough, and hard working. It worked, my brother and I were the first in the family to attend college. My brother Larry became educated in business and I became a doctor.

"There were fun times in the family like the one vacation we got in our entire childhood, the smell of baking cookies from the kitchen, laying on the floor with my dad listening to country music. But the best and the loudest laugh I can remember was when mom got so mad at dad that she squished a banana right in his face. My brother and I were shocked. Smiles off our faces, jaws dropping, never seeing this before. But, when my dad let out the biggest, loudest belly laugh it was a sign that life was back to normal and we all laughed till it hurt. My mom was always a bit atypical and my dad always social and loved people.

My kid time was spent in the neighborhood with about 10-15 guys playing sandlot sports, wandering in the woods with great freedom to roam, and hanging out in the neighborhood park. The one organized sport that I loved was playing tight end for the football team. Life back then was a paradise on earth. What else can I say."

I asked Roger, did you have any idea of what you wanted to be when you grew up? "I always had a need to take care of things, so with my love of animals, mostly dogs and horses, I decided to become a veterinarian."

## Life During the War

Roger had told me earlier that he really didn't support the war in Vietnam, and yet he joined so my first question was why did you join? His answered, "I had never considered joining the military, and in fact I worked really hard in college to avoid being drafted. But I knew that many of those who were in the war had no choice about being there and I wanted them to be given the best care, so I joined up as flight surgeon for the Air Force and for two years I gave the best care that I could and they deserved.

So, you're there and what is going on? "To tell the truth I loved the work, the airmen, their families, the squadron culture, being part of the rescue missions and the combat support missions. My first squadron was C-130, the work horse of tactical air lift, which was tasked to enter areas, with weapons, supplies, and military personnel, in Vietnam and Cambodia where fighting was still pretty high. We would need to land fast, move fast, keep the engines running, deliver the goods and get the hell out of there.

What was it about the airmen that impressed you?

"While, in WWI the average life expectancy of a pilot in theater was 45 days. They lived hard and burned it at both ends. This culture of hard living permeated the fighter pilot culture all the way up and through Vietnam and only changed when the airplanes became so high performance and demanding that pilots needed to be consistently at their best. The mission is demanding and not forgiving. High speeds, high G forces, a mission involving either outmaneuvering enemy aircraft, dropping bombs or both, is a high-risk environment. That's why flight surgeons are critical to ensure pilots are safe to fly and why we fly with them to understand the mission. In my career, we lost many fliers. Some friends.

"But fighter pilots are lively, fun loving, have a great sense of humor, and overall devour life. They are very exciting to be around and I am still in awe of what they do in the air. I have high regard and great respect for these heroes."

"One mission to Cambodia we were delivering weapons and ammunition to a surrounded Phnom Pheh. After landing we were off loading the weapons when an engine quit. We were told to get out ASAP because they expected a rocket attack and minute and we were parked next to the ammo storage area. We could not get that engine going no matter what we tried."

I remember other veterans saying "It is all in luck whether you stay or your gone" so when Roger continued by saying "By luck another of our C-130's landed with supplies, backed up in front of us and jump started our engine with its exhaust. We were able to get out before the rocket attack started." I also remember hearing that luck is a lady but, in this case, I think it was a C-130.

Roger went on to say "I also flew with the HH3-Jolly Green, the work horse for rescue and air evacuation, squadron who would evacuate our injured military to the Philippines. Once evacuated we would transport to nearest hospital.

"One thing that I did experience was to go with volunteers to deliver medical care to remote villages in the Philippines. We traveled with trucks or native boats. I really liked all these missions but still a little nerve racking since they were under martial law then because of terrorist activity and we were with armed guards.

We took a quick breather and then I asked Roger, were you involved in the evacuation of Saigon? He said," Yes, the evacuation began around April of 1975 with Operation Babylift where we evacuated children. I remember one A C-5 filled with kids crashed near the Mekong River killing around seventy-five children and medical personnel. The crazy thing is I was supposed to be on that flight but my radio was malfunctioning and they had to leave without me.

## Life After the War

Tell me a bit about life after the war?

I asked if he could start with a little about family first. Roger began, "As I told you earlier, I was married before I went into the service and my wife and I were having our first child. I had met Paula when she was sweet sixteen and I was just nineteen. She was and is very outgoing, very attractive, very smart and an excellent mother of Jeff and Jennifer, our two children. She could have been anything she wanted to be but she became my wife and an excellent x-ray technician.

As far as my career, after discharge I took my experience from the service as a flight surgeon and went into the field preventive medicine. In other words, keeping people healthy and performing at their best even in high risk environments. I love prevention and became the Chief Flight Surgeon at the Surgeon General's Office in Washington overseeing preventive medicine for the entire Air Force.

I was recruited by a large health-care system in Pennsylvania to head up a major prevention initiative. After three years, I was told I was doing a fantastic job, but my success was hurting revenue. Civilian health care was not as motivated to keep people healthy as the Air Force. Its motivation depended on sickness. I was fired for doing such a good job. That launched me into a career working in, and writing a book on, successful aging. Because the demographic was changing with 10,000 people turning 65 every day and new research showing that lifestyle, not genes, were the major factor in how we age. The great part was I got to work with my brother and with our talents complementing each other we have succeed with a book to tell the story of the research, what we had done, and to motivate everyone to do what the title said...Live Long, Die Short.

## Questions

1. Why do we have wars?
   Because our leaders often fail at diplomacy or have sinister motives. Most wars are either started or prolonged for economic reasons. Greed is the most common, or power, since a war usually gives a president more power and prestige, and usually less criticism (at least in the beginning). For example, Iraq had nothing to do with 9-11 but it was an opportunity to get back at Sadam Hussein who insulted W's father, it was an opportunity to potentially grab lots of oil, it was an opportunity to get support for a failing administration, and an opportunity to make money for Dick Cheney and so many others... Some say that the warnings of the attack on 9/11 were ignored deliberately (I don't know about that). That is sinister.... Vietnam for sure was sinister.
2. What was the role of the media?
   The media is often complicit in beginning and in propagating war; sometime unknowingly as they are used by leaders. The media is often an important part in supporting the end of war.
3. How were women treated?
   The women I worked with were sometimes in danger but usually not. There was a C5 crash that killed many (I was supposed to be on that airplane) but the crash was mechanical, not due to enemy fire. Most of the women I worked with were in health care.
4. Treatment of gay and lesbians?
   I don't know any details, but I suspect, given how being gay was viewed, that they were dishonorably discharged if they had any sexual relations... especially men. I doubt they received benefits.
5. What treatment was there for PTSD?

During the Vietnam war it was called combat fatigue. They were generally kept in theater and returned to duty.

6. <u>How were Black soldiers treated?</u>
   There was a big push to improve racial differences. I'm not sure what drove it, but I suspect that because we had so many African Americans drafted it would have been difficult to have an effective fighting force if we did not fully incorporate them. It was the right thing to do, of course, but I suspect there were other more practical motives.
7. <u>What would you tell young people today about joining the military?</u>
   I firmly believe that mandatory service would be a solution to many problems the country is currently struggling with. Service could be military, peace corps type work, hospital work, civilian support for military, or national parks....etc. Right out of high school, both genders, with no exceptions. You could not apply for college or get a job without having served. At least 18 months but two years probably better.

   It would address the lack of commitment of many college students, it would provide a work force for all kinds of projects, it would allow young adults to understand service for the greater good. It would instill more of a commitment for the values of the US and democracy. I believe it would provide real life experience to young adults which would serve them well in deciding what to do with their lives.
8. <u>Would you do it again?</u>
   I was against the war but never felt as a military person that I should be anything but 100% supportive of the military people fighting. Even though I was one of those Veterans that was spit on when I returned, and even though we were shamefully treated, YES in a heartbeat. However, I would probably not because of the strain on the family.

Do you think even the smartest public can sometime be the dumbest? Just asking.

# CHAPTER 28

## *"Another View" Jane Griffith - Heritage Welsh - Rehabilitation Worker*

**Life Before the War**

So, off I go to find Jane Griffith and see if she would give me the honor of an interview. My first e-mail came back with her answer. "If you're glorifying the war, I am not the person you want to talk to." My response was, "If you believe old congressmen should fight the war and leave the children to grow-up, perhaps we might have something in common." She replied, "You are welcome, come on over." That is how I met Jane, and I was so damned lucky to have such an opportunity as this.

My first impression of her was, how could this petite five-foot frame survive in the middle of a war. She presented with short wavy strawberry blond hair and eyes of blue. Her voice was strong and to-the-point and so we wasted no time.

I asked her to talk a bit about her parents.

She began, "From the very beginning I saw my parents as beautiful, handsome, and smart. They were both teachers, so almost every interaction with us kids would be some kind of exploring of our environment. Growing up with my parents was always an adventure.

"My mother was very athletic. She was realistic, hard-working, optimistic with a fun-loving nature. I believe the hard-working part came when at thirteen her father died, she took on the role of an adult. She began helping her mother with the responsibility of raising her two siblings. When she reached college level, she completed her four-year curriculum in three. This fast pace was in order to work, make money, and pay for her sister's education. I believe from the day she was born she just was one of those people that just cared about people.

"My dad had blue eyes and black thick hair. He had a flair for fine dress. He even wore bow ties and always critiqued the clothes my mother and I wore. He taught at Aleppo College in Syria and he explored the Middle East and Europe during summer vacations. Dad was the more serious one. He had a strong belief in service and openness to all cultures. I think the openness of both parents came from and through their roles as professors and through the opportunity to travel to foreign countries and meet other people, cultures, and learn from them both.

"Because of his travels my dad had the opportunity to make friends in many cultures. Some friends were in the Armenian and Arab community in Boston. He also had friends in the gay community, who would come to visit, which wasn't typical in most 1950-60 suburban homes. People trusted my dad due to his very openness to life."

When asked about her childhood interests, she said, "Since my parents had summers off from teaching, we would go camping and traveling all over. Everyone in the family pulled his or her weight. It was a great way to learn that if you want fun there is responsibility.

"When not travelling, I was at the local library. I love reading and became an avid reader. I read every one of the series of 'Famous Americans' by the age of ten. The one I remember most was the one on Jane Addams. I thought it was due to my first name, but, as I grew older, I found I was following in her footsteps. She had a vision for a better future and became an advocate against the injustice in the world. She advocated for poor immigrants, social justice, woman suffrage. Since then, at the age of ten, I wanted to do something meaningful with my life. I became focused and serious with my vision which was to make things better. Having a goal so young made it hard for me to fit into high school with all the silly girls and cliques. I think from reading and traveling to Europe with my parents, and having a direction of my own, I just felt older and that my horizons were wider than my classmates.

"When I went off to college, I found the same sort of restrictive atmosphere - a bit different this time from the middle-class high school to an all-women's college yet defined by the sameness I had found in high school. Wheaton was full of mostly rich women who had gone to private high schools and had many more advantages than I. It was hard to relate to these women and again I found my comfort in a man's world. I still had my vision and worked hard at classes. I mainly enjoyed dating young men who were in college and debated philosophical topics. I was very interested in other opinions about the world and the people in it.

"It was at this time I met my former husband, David. He was a Dartmouth College classmate of my brother's, who, when I met him, was about to leave for West Africa for the summer. This would be 'my ticket out of Boston.' David and I decided we wanted to be a little deeper in politics and by a quirk of fate while we were interviewing for African positions with the American (Quaker) Friends Service Committee, we were recruited to apply for the position of Directors of the AFSC humanitarian projects in Vietnam.

## Vietnam

I asked if she might first start with her impression of the environment in Vietnam.

She said, "My first impression of going from the rural airport down the packed dirt road to town was that I had arrived on the set for a western movie with horse-and-carts and people on bicycles coming down the street. The tanks that rumbled by and the semi-trucks that screeched their air horns made it abundantly clear I was, indeed, in a war zone. Our simple house, where we all lived, was nestled in amongst Vietnamese houses with no barriers separating us. We walked to work without guards or protection. The lack of 'need for protection' was that I was a member of The American (Quaker) Friends Service Committee, which was established by the Quaker Religion. Just for those who are not familiar the definition of Quaker. It means equal. Its Rehabilitation Center is in Quang Ngai Vietnam because this region was one of the most heavily fought-over areas in all of Vietnam. My Lai village was five miles from the Rehabilitation Center where a staff of westerners –mostly Americans trained Vietnamese in the art of making prosthesis, braces and wheelchairs from bicycle parts. When I arrived in the spring of 1970, the Center had been operating for four years and the Vietnamese staff served about fifty patients a month (the limit only due to the number of beds and workers). Based on the Quaker pacifist creed, our Rehabilitation Center treated all patients regardless of race, religion or political beliefs. In other words, we treated all sides in the conflict. The Vietnamese understood this critical principle. As they often said to us, 'We aren't against the American people, only the government and its leaders.' This attitude and the fact that all the American staff spoke Vietnamese, made a huge difference in how we related to the people. I often felt sorry for the American soldiers who lived in compounds isolated from contact with Vietnamese, except for those who were secretly spying on them or prostrating themselves to the American money, and were unable to speak Vietnamese - to either ally or enemy. Knowing the Vietnamese language was one of my greatest advantages. I had a chance to live and work with Vietnamese which gave me huge insights into their culture. At the same time, I could care and support all victims from the physical and mental pain of the injured from both sides of the war.

"My job was to train the social workers in assessing the patient's potential home environment and work situation and to support what he or she would face when returning home. My knowledge of this process was taught to me by talking and observing our physical therapist. Second priority was to develop a social program for patients and a school at the Rehab Center (mostly for kids of patients - the whole family had to come to care for a patient since there were no meals or evening coverage at the hospital.) The third goal was to determine if the patient was a candidate for a micro loan to help the amputee individual find a new way of life, if they couldn't go back to their former occupation. I would like to note here that every loan AFSC ever made to the Vietnamese former patients was paid in full.

"The other program of great interest to me was our program to provide medical help to prisoners and to the children incarcerated with their mothers. At first, the prisoners were mainly petty criminals but quickly the population of prisoners changed to political prisoners who were jailed for their political beliefs. But in a country, where it was difficult to know who was friend or enemy, most of the prisoners were people thrown into prison to be questioned in order to learn more about the person's political persuasions or possible connections to National Liberation Front (Viet Cong) sympathizers whether fellow villagers or family. Eventually, I discovered that the prisoners I was seeing on the prison ward had first been held in an interrogation center where they were tortured for information. If the officials there felt the patient might die or be seriously ill, they would be transferred to the prison ward on the grounds of the hospital.

Since the Quakers had official permission from the government to treat prisoners in the main prison, we also were given access to the prisoners in a prison ward on the grounds of the provincial hospital.

The prisoners were mostly women who were tortured. It was a 'coming of age' moment for me to realize that the CIA men, who lived in a 'secret' compound in town, were personally torturing the Vietnamese as well as training Vietnamese in torturing techniques. I believed in the general good intentions of my country but this episode woke me to the fact that my country could do evil. I am not saying the enemy did not do the same just that I believed at that time my country could do no evil. Different tortures were allowed such as the Tiger Cage or the Electric Torture."

Can you explain these two types of torture?

She begins with, "The Tiger Cage was designed by the French in 1861 to isolate those, including Buddhist Monks, who were supporting the Vietnamese Independence. The Tiger Cages were boxes about four feet square. The guard walked on ramp between the "cages" and threw what meager food the prisoners received down into the cages to the prisoners. Most of the prisoners were tortured and lost the ability to walk because their leg muscles had atrophied from not being able to stand or walk for so long. The prisoners were 'paralyzed' from the waist down.

"My contact with two prisoners from the Tiger Cages occurred in 1973 after the Peace Accords were signed. There were some prisoner releases on the three sides of the conflict - the US POWs were released from North Vietnam and South Vietnamese prisoners (who had not supported the Saigon Government and fought against the US troops and the Vietnamese soldiers they funded) ---and North Vietnam prisoners held in southern Vietnam were also released.

Two of these political prisoners came to the Provincial Hospital in Quang Ngai and finally came to the Quaker Rehabilitation Center which was on the grounds of the hospital. Neither man could walk. They had fashioned pieces of wood with short legs on them and used these little stools to scoot around on the dirt floor of the Tiger Cages. They each wore a shirt made of patchwork pieces of cloth---mainly scraps of grey and black. As their shirts wore out, they patched them with shirts from other prisoners, sometimes from prisoners who had died. The strong faces and the dignity these men showed was quite impressive. One man was about my age at the time - 29. He had been in jail for all his youth. It is times like this, that the one-on-one confrontation which makes the strongest impression. This man had his youth stolen because he had wanted his country free and independent. He had been in prison the whole time I had been to college, gone on vacations, toured Europe. It just deeply moved me.

The other man was slightly younger. His family came to meet him and I witnessed the 'conflict' of the Vietnam war in the South. His brother came in his ARVN uniform because he was fighting for the Americans. He realized then that his brother was supporting those who were against his cause. But they embraced like any brothers would/should. In time this young man regained use of his legs and went home. What irony though, we restored his legs to function just so that he could walk home and then be blown up near his village."

Tell a bit about electrically torturing?

She looked at me and said, "The cruelty was beyond understanding. It was one of my worst memories watching the female political prisoners who were being held on the prison ward at the provincial hospital, have seizures. The women had been tortured with electricity to their nipples, finger tips, and genitals. It seemed that the electricity did damage to the nervous system causing the women to have seizures. Their bodies would tremble, eyes roll, mouth foam a bit. One cannot imagine how hard it was to see their pain and not be able to totally stop it. It was a torture in itself to just see.

"I went to the hospital to see these prisoners. When I did, the prison guard wasn't the least interested in what I was doing there. He would take the time I was with the prisoners and take a cigarette break. That was good for me because it gave me the opportunity to speak with the prisoners alone, record their stories, and take their photos while the AFSC doctor examined them and dispensed medicine."

This must have been horrible for you to witness.

"Horrors," she said. "The bloodiest scene was probably the day a bunch of kids were brought into the hospital who were wounded from a rocket which hit their school. It was an all-out emergency and I went into the 'closet' of our Rehab Center which was our non-sterile operating room. I helped our doctor Chuck Henkel saw off legs of kids who had been injured. Another scene I remember is going to the Burn Ward at the hospital and helping to change bandages on burn patients. I hated seeing the maggots that were in the dressings. Now science has learned that the maggots eat dead skin and found it helped prevent infection/gangrene, but at the time I did not - and still do not - like maggots. I brought some of the most severely burned patients to Saigon to the Barsky Burn Unit. That was a pretty horrendous place to visit - full of severely burned children. To my amazement, the doctors made tubes of good skin on their bodies -stretched and grew that skin - until it could be grafted over unhealed burn areas.

Oh wait, another thing I wanted to point out as 'worst of the human devastation' were the Agent Orange victims I visited in Quang Nam province in the year 2000. With some money raised on behalf of Dang Thuy Tram - her diary Last Night I Dreamed of Peace - I went to Vietnam to give small amounts of money to victims/families who had been selected by the Quang Nam Agent Orange Help Organization --mostly with the help of my friend Mai. She and the Agent Orange committee identified families who could benefit from a small loan to increase an income to the family of the victim. These children born to parents who were exposed to Agent Orange were horrific. One eye, twisted limbs, only reminders of humans. It was hard to visit and look at these children without turning away.

"It feels hard to write anymore. No matter how long ago, that war stays with you. I'm not even going to re-read this for corrections."

I suggested we move on. We did.

## Life After Vietnam

I asked about her re-adjustment to civilian life?

"Wait," she said, "Just while I am remembering. When I told you of the prisoners and the pictures I took along with their stories. - While we sent the photos of those tortured prisoners back to the Philadelphia Office AFSC these pictures did not even cause a stir. A previous AFSC doctor had testified before Congress about the AFSC staff witnessing the results of torturing but I want you to know neither the public or government seemed to care or show any interest in the situation. They just put it aside.

In 1970 two congressmen, an aide Tom Harkins (who later became Senator Harkins) a US government representative and Don Luce, an interpreter who worked for a nonprofit in Vietnam discovered the Tiger Cages. While they were being given a tour of the island. The Tiger Cages were absent from the list of sites they were supposed to see on their official tour of the island. But Don Luce had been given a secret map of where to find the Cages. Hawkins was shocked at the sights and smells-- and he took pictures --about 500 prisoners--which later he was pressured into handing over to the government officials who were sponsoring this congressional trip. He was warned by one of the Congressmen that the pictures would disappear and Harkins held the copies until July 7, 1973 and then they were published in Life magazine."

Now, back to your re-adjustment. While, she said most of the returning AFSC staff tried to fit into their previous lives and occupations, though a few chose to change directions because of their experience in Vietnam. They returned to school to retrain in various medical fields.

"The previous director before me, became a Buddhist monk and dropped out of mainstream life.

"Things suddenly changed in1973 when I returned to the United States. A photograph of the infamous Tiger Cages was on the front page of Life magazine and there was shock among the public and civil rights advocates. The black and white photos I had taken were enlarged, one appeared in *Time* Magazine and others were used by me when I was interviewed on major television shows, like Good Morning America. For a year after I returned to the US, I was sponsored by Amnesty International (AI) and AFSC to travel across the US, and to Holland, Germany and France to speak about what I had seen in Vietnam and to address the question of torture via a BBC documentary in which I was interviewed called, 'A Question of Torture.

I believe my mental health was saved by having the chance to talk about my Vietnam experiences during the speaking tour. Occasionally I met a hostile audience but mostly people listened. I lived in a war zone for three years, and I was telling them what I had seen and heard. Later, I worked for the Indochina Peace Campaign on a strategy to stop funding the Vietnam war. Vote by vote we lobbied Congressmen (few congress women) and their aides. A genius political operator worked in an office to plan my visits and devise other activities to influence Congress. The cut in funding had a demoralizing effect on the South Vietnamese military and demonstrated the waning support for them by the US government.

Not only was I able to talk about my experiences while I served in Vietnam, but I was able to make an impact on the war itself when I returned. This opportunity was due to The Quakers belief that they do not just serve in times of war but they witness in order to speak truth to power. I was thankful that the three years in Vietnam helped me not only develop friendships with Vietnamese, but an understanding of the issues involved in the war. It gave me the chance to return and share my beliefs and also find a way to heal through speaking and action.

When the tour was finished, I returned to my former career as an art historian and worked in museums and historic preservation, the war seemed far in my past. But then I divorced and no longer had a partner to share war stories and memories with. I felt isolated and sometimes had bad dreams. I had a need to return to Vietnam and try and find some sort of peace. So, in the year 2000 I decided to renew my connections to Vietnam.

"I organized a trip back to Vietnam with four AFSC colleagues and four of our children. Being able to go to North Vietnam seemed incredible but the most memorable time was returning to Quang Ngai to see the former AFSC Rehabilitation Center. The prosthetists we trained were still working at the Center. We shared photos of the old days and were delighted the seeds we had planted were flourishing and even blooming better under Vietnamese leadership (The staff had invented several adaptive prosthetic devices more appropriate for Vietnamese style life than the mainly cosmetic style legs we had offered the Vietnamese).

"The most important part of this trip back to Vietnam was my uniting with my best friend Mai, a woman who lost both her legs by stepping on an American mine, when she was injured in a communist-held territory, Mai was flown to an American airbase where her legs were amputated and she was held as a prisoner.

"She was later released to the Quaker Rehabilitation Center where, after she received prosthesis and learned to walk, she eventually joined the staff at AFSC.

"During the three years we worked together, Mai and I became close friends. Mai spent hours and hours explaining the history of the Vietnamese people, their battle against the Chinese, Japanese and French invaders. Her family all fought against the French and she joined the NLF when she was in high school. Since Mai's mobility was limited, she lived In the AFSC house along with two other former patients who were now staff. They all rode to the Center on motorbikes.

"My loyalty was tested by Mai. Because Mai was not her real name. I never met her family and knew few of the hard facts of her life. I did come to realize that she had sympathies with "the other side" (which is how the Vietnamese in Quang Ngai referred to the NLF/North Vietnamese). Because of that, she was able to help me with communications into areas controlled by the NLF and she was critical to the safety of the AFSC team when the North Vietnamese took over Quang Ngai at the end of the war.

"I could only guess about her role in the war while I worked with her in Vietnam. We lost touch after the war ended and this trip in 2000 was the first time we meet again. There were lots of tears. My daughter accompanied me on this trip and Mai met the daughter who carries (her name Mai) as her middle name. When my son met Mai, he was deeply touched at how two women from different countries at war, different religions, educational and family backgrounds had become such close 'sisters.'

"The war was over and I learned a bit more about Mai's background on this trip but it wasn't until five years later on a return visit that I learned that during the war, she had been the head of public relations (propaganda) for three provinces and a member of the Communist Party. Finally, I knew the truth. Mai was, in the eyes of my government, 'the enemy.' To me she was and continues to be my closest friend. Mai has come to the US to visit me and I have visited her several times as recently as last year.

"As of today," Jane says, "My life advantage is that I seem to be resilient. I believe my strengths like my mother was the ability to possess a joy for living and a strength to endure. Otherwise, life would have crushed me. For example, as I have explained to you, my grandson has a rare genetic disorder. Instead of staying in DC and watching from afar, I moved to Boston and got involved in helping my daughter find the best path for Jack through the government and medical systems. I enrolled in ASL classes at night and took daytime conversational signing classes. I've helped out a lot and now Jack is enrolled in one of the best schools for deaf special needs kids in the country. Now that Jack is in school, I hope to involve myself in other projects."

I do believe the experience of Vietnam made Jane strong enough to handle anything else that comes her way. As of today, Jane continues to advocate for peace in any avenue she finds herself. She is contemplating writing her whole story for publication. She has been published before, and I am not the only one encouraging her to continue.

# CHAPTER 29

*Short answer to a Large Problem*

A Marine, who was enlisted in the service during the Vietnam era heard about this book and the questions that I asked the veterans, he did not want to tell his story but did want to answer a question that I had posed in my interview. It was how are gays treated in the service?

His answer, "At the time nobody was going to know I was gay, EVER, for the rest of my life. I hated me because I was gay. It was drilled into your head right in boot camp that being gay would not only end your service career, it would be very dangerous! They talked about 'faggots' and 'queers' being low-life scum.

"I saw the response to a couple of guys getting caught having sex when I was standing corporal of the guard. I hear the call come over the radio while I was checking sentries. I answered the call and said I was en-route but was told that two other MP's were already there. I went back to the guard shack. As I entered the front door they were coming in the back door, two off duty MPs and three other Marines. The two guys were already bloody and beginning to bruise. The officer of the day still hadn't showed up so I was still in charge. I told the three Marines to leave. I told the other two, one who was starting his shift, to lock the men in a cell. I thought the two guys would be safe in there. The guards put them in a cell but instead of being safe the two guards decided to go in with them. The guards started beating and spitting on them. I had to go in myself to stop them. One prisoner was crying saying he was drunk and the other was just totally silent.

"They got medical attention the next morning and sent to the main base. I'm not sure how long it took, but paperwork came to us stating that they both receive DISHONORABLE DISCHARGES!! Their lives ruined!

"From day one Marines were told homosexuals were scum and were deserving of whatever they got. The Marine Corps Is full of heroes, no doubt, but they also have a lot of hateful and angry and prejudiced fools."

I asked him if he thought times have changed?

"Has it really changed much, I don't know, but I do know that all those ruined lives didn't get to change. Their lives are still ruined."

What do you think?

Just asking.

## Weapons

**The M16 Family**, the most common answer would be the M16A1. It was first introduced in the Vietnam war and was the most common weapon for all soldiers to use during the war. The M16 is most commonly used as a three round burst rifle (meaning it only fires three bullets at a time to give the weapon better range and accuracy) but the weapon can also be used as an automatic weapon as well. Other weapons were the M14 semi-automatic and automatic rifles, M60 machine gun, 50-caliber machine guns, the quad-50 (four 50cal machine guns mounted on the back of a truck with one trigger that fired all of them at once), M79 grenade launcher, Claymore anti-personnel mines

**Colt Commando,** Also in the running for the most popular gun during the war of Vietnam. It is a shortened version of the M16 with a telescoping stock. It has an 11.5-inch barrel in comparison to the M16 with a 20-inch barrel. The Colt Commando was most commonly used by the special operations units that hardly saw the front line during the Vietnam war.

**VC Booby Traps**, they consisted of pressure release grenades that could cause complete obliteration Then there was, the punji pit, a pit with spikes at the bottom covered by leaves. An when a soldier would stumble into the trap the spikes would be covered with the enemy's own excrement. This would poison the wounds. Then there was a pressure triggered rope trap. There were many different variations of this trap but they were all built the same, a soldier would trip the hidden rope, and: set off a grenade, shoot an arrow, or even send a log slamming into soldiers.

**Chemicals- Napalm** Because of the guerilla tactics, the Americans used napalm to literally burn down the forest, this would expose the Vietnamese from any hiding spots. The only problem was napalm back then was very inaccurate and would often reach civilians. Many innocent civilians were killed by inaccurate shots with the napalm strike. The napalm strikes that they used in the Vietnam war were a composition of naphthenic and palmitic acid which caused a giant flammable explosion when hitting the ground. **Agent Orange** is an herbicide and defoliant chemical, one of the "tactical use" Rainbow Herbicides. It is widely known for its use by the U.S. military as part of its herbicidal warfare program. It is a mixture of equal parts of two herbicides, 2,4,5-T and 2,4-D. In addition to its damaging environmental effects, traces of dioxin found in the mixture have caused major health problems for many individuals who were exposed. The diseases now on the VA's Agent Orange list are ischemic heart disease, lung and trachea cancers, prostate cancer, multiple myeloma, Hodgkin's disease, non-Hodgkin's lymphoma, Parkinson's Disease, type 2 diabetes, peripheral neuropathy

## Letter Home

Instead of a letter written by a veteran I decided to put the writings of a veteran of Vietnam who, at this time in life, would rather not do an interview, but gave permission to share these words.

Coming Home

It seems I was just a boy,
Going out to the coast to play.
When they said I had to sign,
That I had to leave today.

Be part of the machine,
We were going to clear the way,
To Freedom in that place,
So very far away.

Reality hit us hard,
This was not a game.
Weeks turned to days,
Days turned to pain.

We countered each day that passed,
Until we could leave at last.
Go back to where we came,
To be ourselves at last.

The World was not what we thought,
What we all dreamed and talked.
Our friends were not the same,
It was just more hate and rain.

I dreamed we won the war,
But the war won us you know.
We lost our way,
How do we get home?

Author Lcpl Dennis Wiehe USMC- Vietnam Veteran
(1969-1971)

# FINAL NOTE FROM THE AUTHOR

When I first started out on this mission of interviewing veterans many friends would ask what was the book to be about? I said, I do not know, they haven't told me yet and when they asked what will the name of the book be? I replied, I do not know they have not told me yet. Well we are at the end of the book and here is the answer.

There seems a consistent thread that goes through the veteran's words, about wars, politics, weapons, biases, and human life. The words go, 'war does not end war, it begets war,' 'stronger weapons may hinder but do not stop war.' 'Individuals, in spite of their gender, color, or culture have become more equal in the military due to their courage, bravery, and proof of equal abilities.' Humans will go forth to protect their beliefs, their homes and their country when they believe it is a justified cause, and are willing to risk life and limb.

There are three things that stayed the same throughout. One: wars are usually concocted by politics, greed, money and power and that they are the root of most wars. Two: it is the young, even before their brain is totally developed, are the ones who do the dying. Three: although the military was ready to desegregate around 1947 the country still continued with the Jim Crow laws and the Green Book Travel Guide until sometime in the sixties.

My question to you is, our young joined or were drafted and they went to war, stayed the course, did the job, paid the price, paid it forward, **could we at least pay it back?**

Thank you for reading this book. May your god bless you and every veteran that has served this country.

# REFERENCES WWI


**Poem**

Author – Major Dr. John McCrae
Title – Flanders Field
Printed ttps://en.wikipedia.org/wiki/In_Flanders_Fields#Poem

**Soldier- Marcelino Serna**

Article-The most decorated US WWI veteran from Texas was actually a Mexican immigrant
Author Editorial Ian Harvey
Published- -Printed- El Paso Times, May 30,2016
Article – The Undocumented Immigrant Who Became a WWI Hero
Author- Rodrigo Ayala
Published - May 24, 2017
Article - Marcelino Serna Became World War I Hero
Author Elena Gomez
Published - Borderlands 23- 2004

**Soldier- Henry Johnson**

Title - History of the American Negro in the Great War, original published 1919
Author – W. Allison Sweeney
Published – 1919

Article- Johnson, Henry
Author- Tony Martin
Published–Oct.,2008, https://doi.org/10.1093/anb/9780198606697.article.2001908

Article – WWI Hero Henry Johnson Finally Receives Medal of Honor
Author – Sarah Pruitt
Published June 2,2015

**Soldier- Charles D. Barger**

Article - On 100th anniversary, remembering most decorated American soldier of WWI,
Author Steven Chapman
Published Lawrence County Records, 312 S. Hickory St., Mt. Vernon, MO,6571211/08/2018

Article- Cora Hubbard — Female Bandit
Author Larry Wood
Published – Missouri and Ozarks History, January 31, 2010

Article- The Staffelbach
Author Larry Wood
Published, Missouri and Ozarks History, January 25,2010
Article – Charles D Barger
Author/ Printed - Wikipedia

**Nurse - Ellen N. La Motte**

The Project Gutenberg eBook (#26884) of Backwash of War by Ellen N. La Motte- www.gutenberg.net

**Videos**

Title-The Century of Warfare, Blood and Mud: Trench Warfare in the West 1914-1918
Published - Time-Life Video, 777 Duck Street, Alexandrea VA 22314
Copyright - 1994 Nugus/ Martin Productions

**Books**

Authors - Jesse Brown and Daniel Paisner
Title - The Price of Their Blood
Published - Bonus Books, 875 N. Michigan Ave., Suite 1416, Chicago, IL. 60611
Copyright 2003 by The Lois Pope Life Foundation
ISBN 2003112767(Library of Congress Control Number) Author - Shari Lynn Wigle
Author Dictionary of American History 2003, wwEncylopedi.com.
Title - Treaty of Versailles
Printed Dictionary of American History Encylopedia.com.
((Boemeke, Nanfred M., et al., eds. The Treaty of Versailles: Cambridge University Press,1998)
Copyright Gale Group Inc.

**Articles**

Author - Rob Ruggenberg
Title - Children of the Great War
Published - The Heritage of the Great War/First WWI914-1918
www.great war.nl/children/children.html
Author - Solomon Lewis
Title - "WWI and Choctaw Code Talkers"
Published Bryan Country Heritage Quarterly P.O. Box 154 Calera, Okla.74730-0153
http://www.choctawnation.com/history/people/code-talkers/code-
Author - Gaz Morris

Title - Hatred and Homosexuality - Queer Men in the First World War
Printed - Vadamagizine.com/features/opinions/homosexuality-first
2-22-2014

Author - Judy G. Russell
Title - Age of veterans in WW 1
Printed - January 24,2012
Published - The Legal Genealogist

## References WWII

### Books

Author Brigadier General Albin F. Irzyx – Veteran of WW II, Korea, Vietnam
Title A WARRIOR'S QUILT OF PERSONAL MILITARY HISTORY
Published Ivy House Publishing Group, 5122 Bur Oak Circle, Raleigh, NC 27612
ISBN 978-1-57197-505-8
Copyright Albin Irzyk

Author Granville Coggs, M.D and Anita Coggs Rowell – Veteran WW II
Title SOARING INSPIRATION (The journey of an Original Tuskegee Airman)
Published N'Lighten Publishing, Inc
Copyright 2012 Granville Coggs, M.D and Anita Coggs Rowell (www.coggs-granville.com)

Author Bill O'Neal –
Title Doris Miller Hero of Pearl Harbor – Veteran WW II
Published Eakin Press, Fort Worth, Texas
ISBN 13-978-1-934645-01-7
Copyright 2007 by Bill O'Neal

Author Herb Wetherwax-Veteran -WW II
Title Counting My Blessings
Published Pacific Historic Parks,1 Arizona Memorial Place, Honolulu, HI 96818
ISBN 978-1-936626-55-7
Copyright 2013 Pacific Historic Parks

Author Kenji Kawano
Title WARRIORS-Navajo code Talkers
Published Northland Publishing Co., PO Box 1389 Flagstaff, AZ 86002-1389
ISBN 0-87358-513-5
Copyright 1990 Kenji Kawano

Author Studs Terkel
Title "THE GOOD WAR"
Published Pantheon Books (division of Random House, Inc., New York, NY
ISBN 0-394-53103-5
Copyright 1984 by Studs Terkel

**References Korean War**

**Books**

*Author-Bevin Alexander*
*Title- Korea, The First War We Lost*
*Published-Hippocrene, Inc. 171 Madison Avenue New York, NY 10016*
*ISBN-0-7818-0808-1*
*Copyright 1986 Bevin Alexander*

*Author-Michael Hickey*
*Title- The Korean War*
*Published-Outlook Press, Peter Mayer Publishers, Inc.*
*ISBN-1-58567-035-9*
*Copyright-1999 Michael Hickey*

*Author-Eric Hammel*
*Title- Chosin*
*Published-Vanguard Press, Inc. 424 Madison Avenue, New York, NY 10017*
*ISBN-0-8`49-0856-X*
*Copyright-1981 Eric M. Hammel*

*Author-William Clark Latham Jr.*
*Title-American POWs in Korea*
*Published-Texas A&M University Press*
*ISBN-13:978-1-60344-073-8*
*Copyright-2012 William Clark Latham Jr.*

**References Vietnam War**

Author Stanley Karnow 1
Title VIETNAM, a history
Published original published: New York: Viking 1983
ISBN 0-670-84218-4hc 0-14-014533-8 pbk.
Copyright WBGH Educational Foundation and Stanley Karnow, 1983, 1991

Author Brig. Gen. Albin F. Irzyk-Veteran
Title UNSUNG HEROES, SAVING SAIGON
Published Ivy House Publishing Group
ISBN13 978-1-57197-488-4
Copyright Albin Irzyk 2003

Author Richard Watkins, Veteran Vietnam
Title No Regrets
Published Bay State Books
ISBN 978-9793629-0=3
Copyright 2011, Richard Watkins second edition

Author - Black Soldiers and edited by Bobby White
Title Black Soldiers Tell Their Vietnam Stories
Published The Beckham Publication Group, Inc. P.O. Box 4066, Silver Springs MD 20914
ISBN 987-0-9848243-5-9

Printed in the United States
By Bookmasters